# IRISH WORDS & PHRASES

# IRISH WORDS & PHRASES

## DIARMAID Ó MUIRITHE

Gill & Macmillan

Gill & Macmillan Ltd
Hume Avenue, Park West
Dublin 12
with associated companies throughout the world
www.gillmacmillan.ie

© Diarmaid Ó Muirithe 2002
0 7171 3372 9

Print origination by Carole Lynch
Printed by AIT Nørhaven A/S, Denmark

This book is typeset in 10/15pt Adobe Garamond.

The paper used in this book is made from the wood pulp
of managed forests. For every tree felled, at least one tree is
planted, thereby renewing natural resources.

A catalogue record is available for this book
from the British Library.

3  5  6  4  2

The author and publishers acknowledge permission from
The Irish Times to include some material from the
author's popular column, 'The Words We Use'.

# CONTENTS

For Gerard Smyth

# PREFACE

It is sometimes said, usually by the Irish themselves or by people of Irish descent, that the best English to be found anywhere on this planet is that spoken in Ireland. This kind of patriotic nonsense would be questioned by any honest Irish person familiar with the richness of the dialects of our neighbours across the Irish sea, yet it is true, as the late John Braidwood of The Queen's University of Belfast used to argue, that Irish speech, especially Irish rural speech, is extremely rich. He found that the most striking parallel between Elizabethan English, the most uninhibited in the history of the English language, and the English of rural Ireland is the sheer delight in language for its own sake.

Our rich rural English is, I am sorry to say, regarded in some quarters as uncouth, impure and incorrect. In my young days as a primary school teacher I was reprimanded by a bishop because my pupils who had presented themselves for Confirmation used the old pronunciation of the words bowl (to rhyme with 'howl'), door and floor (to rhyme with 'boor' and 'flure'); one child's use of *ax* for 'ask' and *cangle* for 'candle' almost gave his lordship apoplexy.

I am not sure how matters stand at the moment. I am glad to hear that many schoolteachers, unlike those of Braidwood's day and mine, encourage the use of dialect in the classroom; the inspector and his friend the clerical manager are not the ogres they were. In literature, too, Seamus Heaney, Tom Paulin, John Montague and others use the rich dialect of the north in their poetic works, echoing, perhaps, the belief of Tyrone man of letters Benedict Kiely, who once remarked that 'in a world so tied up in a tight bundle, language must renew itself from such a variety of sources as was never before available; it must renew itself or die in clichés. But in the long run it is only an inborn taste, afterwards cultivated more by talkative company than by the rules of academies, that will find the living phrase and record it in writing.'

But is the language of Kiely's talkative company, that found in country kitchens and in country pubs, dying out, the victim of the educational system, television, radio, the newspapers and advertising copywriters? Dr Seamas Moylan of The National University of Ireland, Galway, worried about this in the preface to his book *The English of Kilkenny*, published in 1995. His worries are, I feel, unwarranted. In a south Kilkenny public house I recently threw out a sampler of his words to six people in their twenties. There were words unfamiliar to me who had been brought up in the neighbouring Co. Wexford ten miles away, separated from Kilkenny only by the

breadth of the river Barrow. My friends were
familiar with Moylan's words and these were part
of their ordinary vocabulary. I took heart. I take
heart, too, from the letters bearing dialect words
from all over Ireland, sent by readers of my
Saturday column on words in *The Irish Times*.

This little book is just a sampler of the English
currently spoken in Ireland. It contains words that
have been absorbed into Irish English from many
sources – Gaelic, Latin, Old Norse, Norman
French, Scots, and the English dialects; you'll find
here too some trace-elements from Germanic
tongues. I have divided the little glossary into three
sections representing the three main strands of the
English spoken in Ireland, and there is a short
introduction to each section to help you *kitchen*
the words, as they say in Ulster – to help you to
savour them.

SECTION ONE

# ANGLO-IRISH

It is scarcely necessary to point out that Irish, a Celtic language, was the language of the majority of the people of Ireland until a variety of circumstances led to its decline in the eighteenth century, and its near demise in the nineteenth. The variety of English which I call here Anglo-Irish is based on the Irish language.

Irishmen who learned English in the period I speak of had to rely on Irish teachers, whose own English differed greatly from Standard English, and was greatly influenced by Irish. Well into the nineteenth century Irishmen learned their English in the illegal hedge schools; after 1831 they learned it at the hands of the National Teachers, the first of whom were themselves products of the hedge schools. The hedge schoolmasters would have been partly self-taught; this explains an important feature of modern Irish English, a tendency to stress a different syllable from the one found in standard English: we say *discip*line, la*men*table, archi*tec*ture, for example.

In areas where Irish has long ago died out, the influence of Irish is still strong. Professor Alan Bliss pointed out in a Thomas Davis Lecture on RTÉ radio* that this is so 'because English has been handed down from teacher to pupil in unbroken tradition since the days when Irish was still spoken; and in areas where Irish has only recently given place to English, the Irish used is very conservative.' He went on to say something which raised eyebrows in the Department of Education at the time: 'Provided he does not try to ape the speech of others, the Irishman has at his command a form of language which distinguishes him from all other speakers of English, and which accurately reflects the social history of his country.'

It has been necessary for me to invent a quasi-phonetic spelling for some of the words printed below. These spellings will no doubt irritate those who have a knowledge of Irish, but foreign readers will be glad of them.

* Published in *The English Language in Ireland*, ed. D. Ó Muirithe, Dublin, 1977.

---

**A chroí** This is found in literature as **a cree, a chree**. It means 'my heart'. In the anonymous *Sir John Oldcastle*, written about 1600, you'll find 'ahone, ahone, ahone, a cree'; in Richard Head's raunchy play *Hic et Ubique* (1663) a character says 'O yea, between me and God achree'. William Carleton, the nineteenth-century Ulster novelist and short-story writer, has 'Conor achree' in *Fardorougha the Miser*.

**A ghrá** The phrase is still in general use in many country areas. It means 'my love'. This term of endearment has been rendered in English literature as **a gra**, **agra** and **a graw**, the latter being a fairly close quasi-phonetic rendering. The seventeenth-century Thomas Dekker in *The Honest Whore* (1605-30), George Farquhar in *The Twin Rivals* (1702), and our own Gerald Griffin in *The Collegians* (1896) used the phrase. Other terms of endearment borrowed from Irish and used in rural speech to this day are **a lao**, **a leanbh**, **a mhaoineach**, **a mhic**, **a mhilis**, **a mhúirnín**, **a rún**, **a stór**, **a thaisce**, and **a théagair**.

**A lao** This means 'my calf'. It seems to be confined to southern Ireland, where it is common in the English of Cork and Kerry. *Lao* must be transcribed phonetically as [le:], though the Kerry writer George Fitzmaurice wrote the phrase as **elay**. He also has **elaygil**, 'my bright calf'.

**A leanbh** is rendered variously as **alanna**, **alanah**, **alannah**, and for a time the latter was in fashion as a girl's name. I once knew a girl called Alannah Coora, which means 'my fragrant child'; another, an American girl who won a beauty pageant in New York, bore the name Alannahmacree, 'O girl of my heart', God help her.

**A mhaoineach**, 'my darling', was rendered by George Fitzmaurice in *The Pie Dish* (ed. 1969) as **aweinach**. Sometimes you'll hear **a mhaoinigh**, which George wrote as **aweinig**.

**A mhic**, anglicised **avick**, is mac, son, in the vocative. James Joyce in *Finnegans Wake* has it as **a vikeen**, 'my little son'. William Carleton has the expletive **vich na hoiah** in *Phelim O'Toole's Courtship*: 'vich na hoiah, Phelim; do you tell me so?' It was the best he could do with the Irish **a Mhic na hÓighe**, 'Son of the Virgin'.

**A mhilis** was written by Carleton **a villish**. It means 'my sweet'. 'When I rise in the morning, a villish, where will be your smile?' he warbled.

**A mhúirnín** We have a gift for palaver, no doubt about it. How many Irish girls have been addressed by potential seducers as **a mhúirnín**? This has been rendered by the Kilkenny novelist Michael Banim as **a vourneen**. In his novel *Crohoor of the Billhook* (1828), a woman tries to entice a man to stay with her with the syrupy entreaty, 'Pierce, a vourneen, wait, a doocy-bit.' Mrs S.C. Hall, a perceptive Victorian commentator on Irish rural life, but an excruciatingly bad fiction writer, gave us 'I've the world and all of shawls, Peggy avourneen', in *Tales of Irish Life and Character* (ed. 1909). She also has **mavourneen**, incorporating the Irish possessive adjective **mo**, my. 'Oh, blessed be the day when I first saw you, mavourneen', she purred in the same book. Irish-

American mothers have also, I'm sorry to say, given Mavourneen as a name to their daughters in baptism. A friend of mine, a Philadelphia priest, questioned a doting mother about the propriety of this, and was told that Mavourneen was an old Irish name for the Blessed Virgin. Ah well.

**A rún** may be heard still, as **aroon**, even in places where Irish has not been spoken for centuries. It means, literally, 'my secret'. Joyce puns on it in *Finnegans Wake*: 'who goes cute goes siucor and shoos aroun …' The punning is on the line of the song *My Mary of the Curling Hair*, a line of which is *siúl go socair agus siúl a rún*, which means 'walk easy and walk, my secret.'

**A thaisce**, sometimes rendered **a haskey** and the better **a hashka**, means 'my treasure'. Seamus MacManus, the Donegal novelist, left it in the original Irish in *In Chimney Corners* (1899): 'Why, Jack, a thaisce', said his mother, 'it's a dangersome task.' An old friend of mine from Wexford once offered me 'a bang of the latch, a haskey'. 'A bang of the latch' is a *deoch an dorais*, a drink for the road.

**A théagair** survives in some counties, rendered in Anglo-Irish as **ahaygur** or **ahagur**. It means 'my dear'. William Carleton has it in *The Geography of an Irish Oath* (1843): 'Ahagur, that wasn't the way their hard-workin' father an' mother made the money.' The word has also been collected recently in Cork, Kerry, Louth and in north Co. Dublin.

**Abhac na rátha** Lovely as some of our Anglo-Irish endearments are, it must be admitted that we are also very good indeed when it comes to terms of abuse. In a rural Co. Limerick pub I once heard a young woman, annoyed at being pestered by a small man who seemed to think he was God's gift to women, getting rid of him by referring to him as an **outnarawka**. This is a corruption of our headword, which means 'the dwarf of the fairy dwelling'.

**Adag** 'This is a small stack of corn. When the stooks of the corn are fairly dry they make them into adags.' So an informant from the stony grey soil of Monaghan, the late Peadar Ó Casaide, told me.

**Ainniseoir** The word is often spelled **angashore** and can mean both a wretched, sickly person and a mean person. The Irish word is from Middle English *anguisse*, from Old French *anguisse*. The Irish of the south-east brought this word with them to the fisheries of Newfoundland in the eighteenth century, and the people of that province adopted it. In doing so, however, they thought that what they had heard was **hangashore**, a word they still use to describe a lazy wastrel.

**Airneál**, in the north **áirneál**, spelled **aurnaun** or **aurnaul** at times, is a friendly word, and it means a friendly night-time visit to a neighbour's house. Patrick Gallagher, better known as Paddy the Cope, wrote a very good book which he called *My Story* (ed. 1979). In it he described his childhood in Cleendra, outside Dungloe in Co. Donegal, and he had this to say: '"What is an airneál?" said Jane. I said that it was a gathering of all the people of the townland into one house for dancing, singing and storytelling.' In the same book he elaborates: 'In Cleendra most of the kitchens were big, eighteen to twenty feet long by fourteen. All the neighbours gathered into one of the houses each night for an airneál. Old men and women, young boys and girls. After the youngsters would have some dancing the storytelling would commence.' Paddy Gallagher went on to found a thriving co-operative society, although he lacked any formal education. I count myself privileged to have known him.

**Áirneáning** in south Wexford and in east Limerick has a slightly different meaning: work done at night. 'She kills herself áirneáining to feed the children,' a Limerickman once wrote to me. I heard an old Wexford woman complain of life in harder times than these: 'A day's work is enough for a body without **aurnaunin** after it.'

**Amadán** is a very common word. It means a fool. It has been given various spellings in Anglo-Irish literature, **omadhaun**, **omadhawn** and **omadaun** among them. Samuel Lover in his story *Paddy at Sea* has: 'And did you take me for your mother, you omadhaun?' James Joyce in his short story *Grace* has: 'It is supposed – they say, you know – to take place in the depot where they get all those thundering big country fellows, omadhauns, you know, to drill.' Somerville and Ross used the word in their story *Poisson d'Avril*, set in Flurry Knox's domain in west Cork: 'Well, and can't you put the palliase on the floor under it, ye omadhawn.' You'll find the word in use in all four provinces.

**Báinín** The Anglo-Irish **bawneen**, sometimes **bauneen**, will be as familiar to tourists as it is to the natives. It's the Irish **báinín**, literally, 'little white'. A parish journal published in west Mayo by Fr Leo Morahan, *An Choinneal*, says: 'The term is applied loosely now to mean any garment knitted or woven from home-spun white thread, e.g. báinín socks, báinín cap, báinín pullover. The proper use of the word in an earlier generation was the jacket of light material worn by a man.' Somerville and Ross in that marvellous story *Lisheen Races Second-hand* have: 'Maybe you'll lend her a loan o' thim waders when she's rinsin' your bawneen in the river.' And James Joyce in

*Finnegans Wake* talks of 'slooping around in a bawneen and bath slipper'.

**Báirseach** This is angliced *bawrshuck*, a shrew, a loud-mouthed woman, and is common in many rural areas. Patrick Kennedy, the nineteenth-century Wexford folklorist, has this in his *Legendary Fictions of the Irish Celts*: 'I'll get you married to a tay-drinking bawrshuch of a woman.' I've also heard **bawshuk**. Mrs Margaret Thatcher was described to me by a Wexford fisherman as 'a ferocious bawshuk of a woman'. A powerful word.

**Banbh** Piglets are **banbhs** in the Irish countryside. The word has been rendered **bonnive** and **bonham** in Anglo-Irish. J.M. Synge in *The Playboy of the Western World* has: 'and shying clods against the visage of the stars he'd put the fear of death into the banbhs and the screeching sows.' The nineteenth-century Tipperary novelist C.J. Kickham wrote the word as *bonnive* in *Knocknagow*; James Joyce chose *bonham* in *Ulysses*: '… but in the convex mirror grin unstuck the bonham eyes and fatchuck cheekchops of Jollypoldy the rixdix daddy.' The diminutive may be either **bonyeens** or **boneens**. Charles James Lever in *Charles O'Malley* (1841) has: 'What's that you have dragging there behind you?' 'A boneen, sir.' That novel was set in the west. 'Who owns the bonyeens, my brave boy?' asked Patrick Kennedy

from Wexford in *The Banks of the Boro* (1867). By
the way, in cardplaying, the Ace of Hearts is called
'the banbh' in many places in Munster.

**Banshee** The word is from the Irish **bean sí**,
woman of the fairies. She is a being whose wailing
is thought to predict death in Irish families. Maria
Edgeworth wrote of this belief in the early
nineteenth century. She has this in *Castle Rackrent*:
'I warned him that I had heard the very banshee
that my grandfather heard under Sir P's window a
few years before his death.' Yeats mentioned her in
*Fairy and Folk Tales of the Irish Countryside*: 'The
banshee was heard keening around the house.'

I am told that in certain parts of the country
they still believe in this being, and fear her greatly.
She is said to lament only those who have an O or
a Mac in their surnames – people of impeccable
Gaelic stock. This idea has sprung from the ancient
belief that a goddess looks after certain old families.
In the ancient story of *Fraoch*, for example, that
hero's death is announced by the wailing of women
who belong to the Otherworld; in another story we
are told that Brian Boru's death was foretold by the
Munster goddess Aoibheall. The Banshee is heard
more often than seen, but in the accounts of those
who have said that they have seen her, she is an old
woman, combing her hair by the light of the stars
as she keens or laments. One of the narratives that
have become attached to her tells of the finding of

her comb by a man who has heard her wail. He takes it into his house, and the following night he hears her awful wailing outside his window. Picking up the comb with a fire tongs, he pushes it through the open window to her. The banshee takes the comb, but the tongs, when he takes it back again, is twisted beyond repair. The man readily understands, of course, what would have happened to his hand had he presented the comb to her ladyship in the normal manner.

**Bansho** Here we have a Donegal loose woman. The original Irish was a euphemism, **bean seoigh**, literally 'a sporting woman'.

**Barmbrack, barnbrack** or **barneybrack** is a loaf of bread with currants in it. The Anglo-Irish spellings are a disguise for the Irish **báirín breac**, little speckled loaf. For some reason or other, these loaves are bought in the shops and not made at home. They are sought after at Hallow E'en and contain a ring; an unmarried person who is given the slice of the brack containing the ring is certain to be wed within a year. James Joyce in *Clay* has: 'The fire was nice and bright and on one of the side tables were four very big barm-bracks.'

**Bean a' tí**, which has found its way into Anglo-Irish as **banatee** and **vanatee**, means 'woman of the house', *vanatee* being the vocative: a bhean a' tí.

**Binneóg** This is a Leinster and a Connacht headscarf. In some places the word is confined to the headscarf milkmaids wear for reasons of hygiene. The Anglo-Irish form is **binnogue**, first used in literature by Lady Morgan in her popular book *The Wild Irish Girl* (1806). Binnogues, she said, were 'handkerchiefs lightly folded round the brows, and curiously fastened under the chin'.

**Bláthach** is buttermilk. A gross anglicised spelling would be **blawhuck**. It is thought to be the only effective cure for a hangover, by the way. **Bláthach and bruthógs** (q.v.) used to be a favourite snack in Co. Tipperary until recently.

**Booley** is common in placenames. It is the Irish **buaile**, which in this era of the milking parlour has become redundant. The booley was a milking place in summer pasturage. P.W. Joyce in his *English As We Speak It In Ireland* (1910) wrote: 'A temporary settlement in the grassy uplands where the people of the adjacent lowland village went during the summer with their cattle, and milked them and made butter, returning in autumn, cattle and all, to their lowland farms to take up the crops.' I've seen the remains of one of these booleys in the Galtee mountains; a cluster of ruins enclosing a grassy field, a monument now, worthy of preservation.

**Bow** The banshee is called **The Bow** (to rhyme

with 'how') in south Kildare, Carlow, south Wicklow, and Wexford; and as the **boheenta** (Irish **badhbh chaointe**, or keening badhbh) in Kilkenny and south Laois. The **badhbh** was originally a goddess of war and as such she plays a strong role in medieval literature. The original meaning of the word was 'scald-crow', and in this form the bloodthirsty goddess used to appear to feast on the corpses of the slain. To call a modern-day lady either a banshee or a bow is a grave insult, as you can imagine. Dr Patricia Lysaght has written the definitive study of the lady. Lady? Well, I'd better say so, as my Wexford grandmother, who firmly believed in her, used to tell me to mention her with respect – just in case.

The Bow is called **The Babow** in parts of Co. Westmeath. Children used to be threatened, 'Be home before dark or The Babow will get you.' You'll also hear the compound **badhb chaointe**, spelled **bocheentha**, in Michael Banim's *Crohoor of the Billhook* (1828): 'The mournful wail of the bocheentha, come to predict the sudden death of himself, or some dear member of his family.' The compound means 'the keening banshee'.

**Boxty** can still be had in at least one Dublin restaurant. It is a kind of bread made from grated raw potatoes and flour, according to the *English Dialect Dictionary*. Simmons, in his late nineteenth-century glossary of south Donegal words, says that 'the grated potatoes are squeezed dry through a cloth, the remainder is baked into a cake, about as heavy and indigestible as a boiled slipper.' Nobody is sure where the word came from.

**Bríc** There are many words for different types of bread in rural speech. **Bríc** (I've seen it written **breek**), is shop-bread. The diminutive is **brícín** (*breekeen*). The word is found in Kilkenny, Tipperary and Limerick.

**Brúitín** An Ulster dish, found in the forms **bruteen** and **brutheen**. This is a dish of mashed potatoes mixed with butter and onions. H.C. Hart, a collector of Donegal words who flourished towards the end of the nineteenth century, wrote of 'bruteen and butter – Irish cheer at old-time weddings. Not much heard of now.' Well, maybe not at weddings, but it is still given to children, and with a glass of milk to wash it down it can be a very palatable and nourishing dish.

**Bruth fá thír** Not by farming alone did many country people live. Some had recourse to the sea, and in places along the western seaboard **bruth fá thír**, which I have seen written as **bru faw heer**, was often valuable to poor people. The word means sea wrack, or as Fr Morahan of Louisburgh, Co. Mayo, put it in his parish journal *An Choinneal*: 'Something washed ashore. It refers not to seaweed or such natural growth, but to such things as timber, rubber, barrels of oil or other fuel, which occasionally are washed on to the shore, especially in the west wind. The clear or coloured glass ball-floats for fishing nets, which have been collected on the shore and used as ornaments, are good examples of *bruth fá thír*.'

**Bruthóga**, or **bruhogues** in an Anglo-Irish disguise, are roast potatoes.

**Buaileam sciath** Written **boolamscheech** by Michael Banim in his novel *Crohoor of the Billhook* (1828), it is, I think, a splendid descriptive phrase. Literally it means 'let us beat (our) shield'; it is used of a braggart. A Limerickman once said to me: 'There's not much to that fellow. All talk and no action, an oul' buaileam sciath.' Banim wrote of 'the rustic boulamscheech, whose glory was gathered by fighting at fairs and patterns, and drinking inordinate potations of bad beer, in hedge ale-houses.' I can vouch for the fact that the word is still used in Kilkenny and in all the counties of Munster.

**Caiscín**, or **cashkeen** as I've seen it written, is a loaf of home-made brown bread. *An Choinneal* informs me that 'it really means the bread baked from home-grown wheat brought to the mill to be ground.' Home bread in every sense of the term.

**Císte** is the Irish for cake; **cístín** means 'little cake'. I love the term **cístín baise**, rendered into

Anglo-Irish as **keeshteen bosha**. **Bas**, Anglo-Irish **boss** and **bosh**, is the palm of the hand, and the delicacy is a little cake made on the side of the griddle especially for a child who is 'helping' her mother with the baking.

**Cladhaire** This is common in its Anglo-Irish form **klyra**. It was described in an article in *An Choinneal* as 'a rogue', in that gentlest and most smiling sense. So it is often used in the vocative to someone who has tried to play a trick on the speaker. Or in card-playing: 'Get away, you cladhaire, you won't fool me.' In south-west Cork it is a ruffian, a rogue; and a Limerick correspondent of mine described a *klyra* as 'a false cut-throat; a spineless coward'.

**Cliabh** has Anglo-Irish forms **cleave, cleaf, tleev**; a diminutive **claven**, and a plural **clavees**. It is a basket, a creel. The form *cleave* is found in the anonymous *A Dialogue Between Teague and Dermot* (1713): 'Some butchers say dey did not leave one fellow dat vou'd carry a cleave.' The north Co. Dublin wordsman Paddy O'Neill called it a **cleaf**. They stored potatoes in it in Fingall. **Tleev** is a Westmeath form. The Tyrone word **claven** is the diminutive of this, in Irish **cliaibhín**. The Monaghan word **cleaver** is from the Irish **cliabhaire**, a man who carries a basket; hence 'a poultry dealer who used to come from

Crossmaglen carrying baskets', as the late Peadar Ó Casaide, a scholarly man from Drumin, Carrickmacross, told me. The plural **clavees** I heard in Co. Cavan and in Co. Louth.

**Cloodogue** is an Anglo-Irish form of **clúideog**. The word was defined for me by a Monaghan woman as a batch of Easter eggs. 'The eggs were covered with straw and hidden around the farm, giving the children a good deal of fun in tracking them down,' she explained. There was, and I'm glad to say, still is, a party connected with the above. It is the children's Easter feast. My good lady from Monaghan went on in her letter to me: 'We always had our cloodogue in our Granny's on Easter Sunday. It consisted in lighting a fire, usually in the paddock where there is a hill, boiling eggs which my aunt had previously painted, and rolling them down the brae. There was lots of tea and sweets and sweet cake, and there was wine and whiskey for the grown-ups.'

**Clúracán**, who appears in the English literature as **clooricaune**, is a mischievous elf. Crofton Croker in his *Fairy Legends and Traditions of the South of Ireland* (1862) has this to say about him: 'A fairy having the appearance of a tiny old man, supposed to have a knowledge of buried treasure, and to haunt wine cellars.' He was also well-known for stealing butter from country dairies at night, and I can attest to the fact that some of the older people of West Muskerry, on the Cork-Kerry border, firmly believed this as late as the 1950s. But where did this little being originate? As far back as the eighth century we find reference to a community of small beings who lived in the time of Fearghus Mac Léide. These people had magic powers, as King Fearghus found out when he captured three of them, and was given the power of swimming as well as any fish in sea or river when he released them.

Folklorist Professor Dáithí Ó hÓgáin wrote that subsequent literary sources also make them bestowers of magical objects, such as a mantle or a pair of silver-bronze shoes which enable a person to travel in water without drowning. 'These', he says, 'are Irish adaptations of international motifs concerning objects which provide for magical travel or magical finance. It is therefore obvious that the designation *lúchorpán* was invented in Ireland when lore of dwarf-communities was adopted from abroad by Irish writers, and that the solitary *leprechaun* (q.v.) of folklore is a post medieval development from the literature.'

**Cóisir**, found in the forms **cosher** and **coshur**, is 'a friendly visit to a neighbour's house', in Co. Donegal. Hence **coshering**, visiting a neighbour's house. Swift has this in *A Dialogue in Hybernian Stile*: 'He sometimes coshers with me.' A *cosher* in Waterford and in Wexford is a house party, and in south Wexford it once had the specific meaning of a children's Easter party. I was told that on Easter Sunday children used to go from house to house asking for eggs. 'Could you spare an egg for my cosher, mam?' Gentler times.

**Colcannon** The potato, of which Thackeray once said that it should replace the shamrock as the national symbol, was an ingredient of this favourite dish. It is rarely seen on the menus of Irish restaurants and more's the pity. It is a mixture of boiled potatoes, chopped leeks and kale. The Irish original was **cál ceanann**. *Cál* is from English *kale*, from Old Norse *kal*, a cabbage. *Ceanann* means 'speckled with white'.

**Collops and spades** It is scarcely credible that in these days some of the old forms of land measurements are still in use. I'm not talking about miles and furlongs, but of things like *collops* and *spades*. I can assure you that there are parts of west Cork and Kerry where these two terms are still in use. A spade is a translation of the Irish *rámhainn*; potato drills are still measured in spades. A *spade* is five feet. *Collop* is the Irish *colpa*. It was the unit for grazing animals. The Tailor of Gougane explained it in his own inimitable way in Eric Cross's book *The Tailor and Ansty*: 'Well, collops was the old style of reckoning for land, before the people got too bloodyful smart and educated, and let the

Government or anyone else do the thinking for them. A collop was the old count for the carrying power of land. The grazing of one cow or two yearling heifers, or six sheep or twelve goats or six geese and a gander was one collop. The grazing for a horse was three collops.'

**Comhar** Where the farms were small and the land poor people shared farm implements and horses to get the work done as quickly and efficiently as possible. They had a word for this, **comhar**, anglicised as **coor** or **core**. You could define it as cooperation; work given as a sort of loan to be paid back, I suppose. Dr Patrick Henchy, the Clare scholar, gave me this gloss: 'They were working *in comhar*, helping each other in turn.' P.W. Joyce wrote from the lush lands of Limerick: 'I send a man *on core* for a day to my neighbour: when next I want a man he will send me one for a day in return. So with horses: two one-horse farmers who work their horses in pairs, borrowing alternately, are said to be *in core*. Very common in Munster.' Yes, and in Leinster as well. The word is from the Middle Irish *comar*, co-tillage, ploughing partnership.

**Créadóir** This has been given as **crayadoor** in a quasi-phonetic Anglo-Irish spelling. It means a potter. But in Louisburgh, Co. Mayo, according to Fr Morahan's parish journal, *An Choinneal*, 'here it is used for a lounger – one who sits down most of the day, just as an olden-time potter had to remain seated at his work. "The lazy créadóir", or "Sitting down all day in his créadóir". Note that *in his* is a direct translation of the Irish *in a*. A standard English version would have "Sitting down all day as a potter would."'

**Crivling** is a Donegal word, one I heard from my late wife. It is an interesting verb, as it derives from an Irish phrase, not a single word. The phrase is **ag cur uilinn air**, which means 'putting an elbow or an angle on it'. My wife's gloss was 'building a turf rick in such a fashion as that the sides are slanted, like a pyramid'.

**Crubeen** is a form of the Irish **crúibín**, a pig's foot. Once considered a delicacy, it was a favourite late-night snack in public houses before the arrival of the Englishman's fish-and-chips in the 1950s. Crubeens were also sold in tents at fairs and races in my youth, as they were a little earlier in the days of Somerville and Ross. In their story *A Misdeal* there is a reference to 'vendors of crubeens, alias pigs' feet, a grizly delicacy peculiar to Irish open-air holiday making'. James Joyce in *Ulysses* mentions that 'Florence McCabe takes a crubeen and bottle of double X for supper every Saturday'. You can still buy the things in places. I saw them being sold at Ballinasloe Fair, in Co. Galway, a few years ago, in a tent where the writ of the European Union on hygiene did not run, I fear.

**Crúiscín** This is another homely word from the Irish farmsteads. It means a little jug. It takes the form **cruiskeen** in Anglo-Irish. *An Cruiskeen Lawn* is the title of a traditional song. It means the full little jug. 'There he is, says I, in his gloryhole with his cruiskeen lawn,' wrote Joyce in *Ulysses*.

**Currach** Where you'll find *bruth fá thír* (q.v.) you'll undoubtedly find currachs, sometimes spelled **curraghs, corrraghs** or **curaghs**. These are light coracles used on the western seaboard. These delicate craft are often mentioned in literature. J.M. Synge in his masterpiece *The Playboy of the Western World* has: 'I've nice jobs you could be doing – gathering shells to make a white wash for our hut within, building up a little goosehouse, or stretching a new skin on an old curagh I have …' Joyce in *Finnegans Wake* did not attempt an anglicised spelling. He left it as *curach*.

**Dailtín** This has given Anglo-Irish **dalteen**. I once asked people from various Irish counties what the word meant to them. 'An impudent young pup', said a man from west Cork. 'A well-dressed good-for-nothing', answered a Limerickman. A Co. Carlow friend gave this gloss: 'You'd hear young fellows calling young women and girls dalteens; stuck-up posers.' The word was originally

from Irish *dalta*, a fosterchild. The diminutive was
first applied to a horseboy, from which it has
drifted to its present meaning.

**Deileadóir** In its Anglo-Irish form this is
**deladore**. It is, according to *An Choinneal*, 'a
complainer, of any size or age or state in life. The
kind of person who has the complaints lined up so
that when one source of complaint is removed he
has another ... and another ... and another.'

**Doirb** In the lost Irish of Co. Leitrim, this was
a waterbeetle. But in the county's English it is
sometimes spelled **dirrib**, and it has come to mean
a sly, spiteful woman.

**Drootheen** To be called a *drootheen* by a
woman in Co. Waterford would embarrass a man
greatly. An interesting word this, from the Irish
**drúichtín**, 'little, or light dew'. The Irish word also
gave its name to a snail, a slug without a shell.
Crofton Croker, in his *Fairy Legends and Traditions
of the South of Ireland* (1862), tells us of a tradition
that has survived to this day: 'A small white slug or
naked snail is sought by young people on May
Morning, which, if placed on a slate covered with
fine dust or flour, describes, it is believed, the
initials of their sweethearts.' Many words are given
figurative meanings, and in this case the *drúchtín*
or *drootheen*, on the lips of an earthy Waterford
woman, would mean a diminutive penis.

**Dulamoo** A noun, it is the Anglo-Irish version of the Irish verbal noun *dul amú*, literally 'going astray'. To be called *a dulamoo* in south-east Wexford would imply effeminacy.

**Easóg** The Anglo-Irish version is **assogue**. *Easóg* is the Irish for a stoat. In west Cork and in Monaghan it has come to mean a spitfire of a woman.

**Feic** Its Anglo-Irish form is **feck**, an object of derision. 'You're only a feck, poor man,' I recently heard a young one taunt her boy-friend who had indeed made quite a feck of himself murdering a tearful ballad in a pub. The Irish *feic* means 'a sight'.

**Fóisí** This has given **foshee** (the *o* is long), a derisive word in Co. Kilkenny for a man who works in fits and starts; in south Tipperary he is a loiterer, a lay-about, and in the words of one informant of mine, 'an inquisitive person, a cabin hunter who comes uninvited for something to eat, or to drink and gossip.'

**Fostúch** This is anglicised **fostook**, a grown youngster, a boy of employable age. That seems to be the primary meaning, but it is now a term of abuse from counties as far apart as Kilkenny and Kerry, where it has come to mean a big, clumsy, idle young man.

**Glig** Originally it meant a bell, and its diminutive **gligín**, or in its Anglo-Irish forms **gligeen** and **gliggin**, has come to be used figuratively, while the original meaning has been largely forgotten. A west Corkman who told me he knew no Irish, but whose English was decorated with thousands of Irish words that he considered English, told me that 'A glig is a woman who can't keep her mouth shut, always ready to talk about things she knows nothing about. We'd say a "gligeen", too.' In both Donegal and Tipperary, a *gligeen* or *gliggin* can be either male or female. Peadar O'Donnell in *The Knife* (1930) has this from Donegal: 'They won't let a priest near us except gligins like themselves.' A Tipperary friend explained that 'a gligeen is a person who babbles nonsense, mostly.' I've also come across the compound **glig glag** for silly talk in west Cork.

**Glincín** I suppose that this word, anglicised **glinkeen**, is related to **glig** (q.v.). A glinkeen has been described to me by a Co. Clare friend as 'a rattle-brained person'. The great *English Dialect Dictionary* says that the word is 'a depreciatory word used of a girl'. Patrick Kennedy, the Wexford folklorist, has 'Such a glinkeen of a girl' in his *Evenings in the Duffrey* (1869). The word has also come to mean a gossip in many counties. 'She have (*sic*) the news of the country, that glinkeen,' a west Corkman told me.

**Gombeen; gombeen man** A well-
known term of insult. He is a usurer, a money-
lender at exorbitant interest. His heyday was in the
nineteenth century. There are many references to
him in literature. Somerville and Ross in *The
Finger of Mrs Knox* have: "'I suppose that's Goggin,
the gombeen?", said Mrs Knox; "how were you
fool enough to get into dealings with him?"' Bram
Stoker, famous as the author of *Dracula*, has this in
his other novel, *Snake's Pass* (1891): 'A gombeen
man is it? He's the man that linds you a few shillins
or a few pounds … and then niver laves ye till he
has tuk all ye've got.' James Joyce in *Ulysses* refers to
'a certain gombeen man of our acquaintance'. The
word's Irish origin is **gaimbín**, diminutive of
**gamba**, a bit, hunk, dollop, which is thought to
derive through the medieval Latin *cambium* from
an unattested Celtic word *kmbion*.

**Grá mo chroí** is another term you'll still
hear in districts where Irish has not been spoken
for generations. It means 'love of my heart'. It has
been incorporated into the English of Ireland as
**gra-ma-cree** and **gra macree**. The word was first
used in literature in the anonymous *Pugatorium
Hibernicum*, written between 1670 and 1675: 'For
old acquaintance, for it's dee/ Dat is mee only gra-
ma-cree.' Carleton spelled it *gra macree* in *Phelim
O'Toole's Courtship*. But my friend Dr Patrick
Henchy, scholar and librarian, pointed out to me

that in Clare 'a grá mo chroí man' is a plausible
fellow, and that *grá mo chroí talk* is soft talk,
*plámás*, flattery. Maggie Purcell from Tipperary
knew of a similar usage. 'It's all grá mo chroí with
him, and nothing behind it.'

**Gráinseachán** I often wonder does anybody
at all nowadays make what were considered
culinary delicacies not so long ago. I'm thinking of
those cheap, nourishing dishes such as
**gráinseachán** and **grán bruite**. *Gráinseachán*,
spelled **graanshaghaun** by P.W. Joyce and
**graunshakaun** by others, seems to be a dish
confined to the southern counties. Joyce, a
Limerickman, says: 'In my early days what we
called graanshaghaun was wheat in grains, not
boiled, but roasted in an iron pot held over the
fire, the wheat being kept stirred till done.'

**Grán bruite**, literally, boiled grain, is found
in the forms **graanbroo** and **brootheen**. P.W. Joyce
described the dish as 'wheat boiled in new milk
and sweetened; a great treat to children, and
generally made from their own gleanings or
liscauns [Irish *lioscáin*] gathered in the fields'.

**Kalish** In its Irish form this is **ceailis**, 'a big, fat
useless woman' in west Cork. A **kalishogue** was
described to me by a Limerick correspondent as 'a
plump young blowen'. A *blowen* is a good-looking
young woman.

**Keening** This is no longer a part of Irish funeral customs. It died out, due to clerical censure, towards the end of the nineteenth century. The original Irish word was **caoineadh**. Keening nowadays means simply crying, wailing; only small children and dogs are told nowadays to stop keening. Here it is, described by Mr and Mrs Samuel Carter Hall in their splendid account of Ireland on the verge of the calamitous Great Famine, *Ireland, Its Scenery and Character*: 'They (the keeners) rise with one accord and, moving their bodies with a slow motion to and fro, their arms apart, they continue to keep up a heart-rending cry. This cry is interrupted for a while to give the bean chaointe, the leading keener, an opportunity of commencing. At the close of every stanza of the dirge the cry is repeated, to fill up, as it were, the pause, and then dropped; the woman then again proceeds with the dirge, and so on to the close. The keener is usually paid for her services, the charge varying from a crown to a pound, according to the circumstances of the employer ... It often happens, however, that the family has some friend or relation, rich in the gift of poetry; and who will for love of her kin give the unbought eulogy to the memory of the deceased ... The dramatic effect of the scene is very powerful: the darkness of the death chamber illumined only by candles that glare upon the corpse, the manner of repetition or acknowledgment that run round when the keener gives out a sentence, the deep yet suppressed sobs of the nearer relatives, and the stormy, uncontrollable cry of the widow or bereaved husband when allusion is made to the domestic virtues of the deceased – all heighten the effects of the keen; but in the open air, winding round some mountain pass, when a priest or person greatly loved or respected is carried to the grave, and the keen, swelled by a thousand voices, is borne upon the mountain echoes – it is then truly magnificent.'

**Kesh** I've heard a fat woman being described thus in Limerick. This is an Anglo-Irish form of céis, a sow.

**Kish** I must confess to the larceny of a **kish** from one of the corners of a ruined hovel in a Galtees *booley* (q.v.). It had been left behind God only knows when – perhaps a century ago – and it was in a remarkably good state of preservation. A **kish** – Irish **cis** – was described in *Paddiana*, an engaging book on Irish life published in 1842, as 'a large oblong basket, commonly placed upon the rude country cart, and used in bringing in baskets of turf from the bog'. There are many references to this kish in literature. The Edgeworths in their *Essay on Irish Bulls* (1830) refer to a Longfordman whose companions left their cars loaded with kishes of turf, and James Joyce quotes a well-known Irish saying in *Ulysses*: 'ignorant as a kish of brogues'. *Brogues*, from Irish *bróg*, are shoes. The diminutive, **kishaun**, Irish **ciseán**, is still very common in Irish speech.

**Klatch** A Co. Monaghan word this for a slut, a trollop. It is the Anglo-Irish form of the Irish **claitseach**.

**Leanán Sí** The spirit the Halls called the **Lanian Shee**, *Leanán Sí* in Irish – Fairy Lover – was a benign Otherworld being who fancied poets and inspired them.

**Leprechaun** There are many kinds of Otherworld beings. The most common is the **leprechaun**. The best-known stories concerning this little rogue relate to his immense wealth in gold, hidden, of course, in the rath or *lios* (q.v.). You'll remember *Darby O'Gill and the Little People*, Disney's engaging film. The leprechaun is, however, and in contrast to King Brian of the film, a solitary being, sometimes shoemaker to the fairies. This is what *The Century Magazine* wrote about him in 1900: 'A lhifrechaun or leprechaun is a fairy shoemaker. If the reader has ever the good luck to catch him, then, having the presence of mind not to remove his eyes from him for a fraction of an instant (thereby rendering the little fellow powerless of melting into thin air), he must at once command him to disclose where there is a crock of gold hid. The little scoundrel will first endeavour to trick you into lifting your eyes off him, and, failing in this, will try fifty little dodges; but finding all useless, will discover to you what you want, on condition of being set free.' The little fellow is known as the **loughreyman** in Ulster. This is the Irish **luchramán**, described to me by folklorist and wordsman Willie O'Kane from Dungannon as 'an elf or sprite traditionally believed to inhabit woods and notorious for stealing money'.

Folklorist Professor Dáithí Ó hÓgáin said of this Ulster sprite in his magisterial book *Myth, Legend and Romance, an Encyclopaedia of The Irish Folk Tradition* (1990): 'He has to an extent become assimilated to the brownie lore, which seems to have arrived from Scotland in the seventeenth century. These accounts have him, or a brownie, coming secretly at night to do farmwork and housework for people to whom he is well disposed, but he leaves in a huff when a suit of clothes is left as a present for him. In Munster the leprechaun is sometimes said to present people with **sparán na scillinge** (purse of the shilling), which never becomes empty. However, those in receipt of this marvellous gift invariably misuse it, and find that its contents change to dust.' The word **leprechaun** was used only in the north Leinster area. In east Leinster the word, Dr Ó hÓgáin tells us, was **loimreachán**, in south Leinster and in Connacht

**lúracán**, and in Munster **luchragán**, **lurgadán**, and **clúracán**. 'All of these designations are suggestive of his traits – echoing terms such as *luch* (mouse), *lúth* (agility), *lurga* (ankle), and *lom* (sparse).'

**Lios** Walt Disney knew of the fascination of the Irish with the world of the fairies, and *Darby O'Gill and the Little People*, based on the little men who inhabit the **lios**, anglicised as **liss**, fascinated the world outside Ireland as well. I well remember that when the film was first shown in Ireland, many of the Dublin critics seemed to be affronted by the notion that Irish people still believed in the existence of fairies. 'Stage-Irish tripe', they said, ignorant of the fact that in the 1950s there were places where the belief in the Otherworld was as strong as the belief in the Christian Heaven.

The linguist Dr R.B. Breatnach of The National University of Ireland, Dublin, went to visit an old man in Ring, Co. Waterford, who was seriously ill. Looking out the window onto a field where some cattle grazed around a ring fort, popularly thought to be a fairy dwelling, the old man said, 'It won't be long now until I'll be enjoying life among them.' He was convinced that the *lios* was a sort of half-way house between here and heaven, where the souls of decent people would stay in the company of the Good People until the last trump sounded. He obviously did not believe in Purgatory. He expected a life of ease and pleasure, with plenty of storytelling, the company of beautiful fairy women, and the best of food and drink.

**Pooka** The **púca**, often spelled **pooka** or **phooka** in literature, is an evil being; much more dangerous than Shakespeare's **Puck**. He often takes the form of a coal-black horse in both Irish and English folklore, which may explain why black horses are often described in the thoroughbred stud-books as 'brown', not black. He may be seen snorting fire as he roams the Irish countryside seeking victims, offering them lifts home on his back, and then dumping them over cliffs and into rivers. Seumas MacManus, in his book *Bold Blades of Donegal* (1937), warns that 'The púca is the one only evil spirit to be met with in Ireland. He is of a shadowy, dark, indefinite form, set low as if he went on all fours ... Always it is on his back that he tries to carry off his unfortunate victim. And woe to him that takes the púca's ride.'

Mr and Mrs S.C. Hall, authors of the 1840s' *Ireland, its Scenery and Character*, were fascinated by the Pooka. They visited the waterfall of Poul-a-Phooka (Poll a' Phúca, the Pooka's Hole), near Blessington, Co. Wicklow, 'which terminates in a whirlpool of unfathomed depth and where, it is said, the famous spirit horse holds its nightly revels, luring unhappy wayfarers into the frighful vortex formed by the waters of the cataract. Its summit is crossed by a bridge of a single arch, with a span of sixty five feet.' They heard many stories about the infamous Pooka, and you'll still hear similar stories to this day from the older people in west Cork. Near Bantry an old man told the Halls of a friend who was going home one night through a dark lonely pass. 'He heard a horse coming along at a fast gallop and drew up to let him pass, when he heard a voice by his side say, "Lien (that is 'lie down'), here's the Pooka coming." And sure enough he saw the beast with his eyes and nose flashing out fire. So the boy turns around and says, "Who are you?", thinking it was a fellow Christian that gave him the warning. "I'm the Lanian Shee" (see *Leanán Sí*), says the voice. Now wasn't it queer that the spirit should be afeared of the Pooka, but you see, they weren't friends at all.'

**Preclechaun** Irish has not been the mother-tongue of mid-Tipperary people for quite a while, but many Irish words survive in the people's English. This is one. The original Irish word was **preicleachán**, and it means a sour, discontented person. The word, I think, comes from Irish **preiceall**, which people from that region have sent to me in the quasi-phonetic spelling **preckle**, and it means both a double chin and a discontented appearance. 'He had a preckle on him all day', was a gloss I got. The word is related to **sprochall**, a person with loose flesh, which gave Anglo-Irish **spruckle**; and you'll have to go back to Roman times for its ultimate origin, the Latin *spiraculum*.

**Priompallán** is the Irish for dung beetle. I've seen it spelled **primpullaun**. It is a beetle which can fly, and this explains the gloss given to me by Dr Patrick Henchy from Clare. 'And hence', he wrote, 'a man who acts socially beyond his station, flies too high and is destined to fall.'

**Prúntach** Many's the time I've heard this word in the English of the west. A quasi-phonetic spelling would be **proontach**, the 'tach' bit to rhyme with 'lough', a lake. It is one of hundreds of words for a fat person. I'm indebted to the Louisburgh, Co. Mayo, parish magazine *An Choinneal* again: 'A fat person, but that's only half the story. The prúntach is so fat and bulky that she (note! she) deserves a page to herself. The very sound of the word suggests excess avoirdupois impinging (by the laws of gravity) upon a soft or delicate mass of matter. Add to this the adhesion of the mass to folds upon folds of heavy woollen or serge material, and here you have the quintessence of prúntach-hood … You are driving to town and on the rear seat of the car you have left the special apple-pie which your mother sends to her daughter-in-law. Thomas's wife wants a lift; she sits in, says "Thanks be to God!" and … then you remember! The prúntach!'

**Pulling the katchee** A *slíbhín* (q.v.) would, I fancy, be given to doing this occasionally. This is a phrase I heard from a Co. Monaghan woman. She was speaking about somebody given to flattery and fawning. *Katchee* is a corruption of the Irish **céad dlaoi**, the forelock (*céad* means first; *dlaoi* is lock or tress). This phrase is also found in Cavan and Louth.

**Punann** What woman wouldn't be delighted to be called a punann? *Punann* is the Irish for a sheaf of wheat, barley, or oats; and to an incurable romantic like myself it conjures images of a lovely golden head, a perfect symmetrical body, a slim waist … A man from Co. Waterford sent me the word; I had heard it before but had forgotten it. My friend spelled it **punnin**, a good guide to the Irish pronunciation. He was in a bar one night in the town of Cappoquin. A tired and emotional member of the farming class was looking at that great comedy *Some Like It Hot* on television, and he became overcome by Marilyn's sexual appeal as she sang that song. He called her the most lovely *punann* he had ever seen and he didn't care who knew it. I'm quite sure that poor Marilyn would have liked the word. The actor Niall Tóibín said to me when I told him the story, '*Punann*, of course, is the lowest form of wheat.' Nice pun, isn't it?

**Rabhdlamán**, rendered **rowdlamaun** in Anglo-Irish, has a great sound to it. It has a specific meaning: a well-meaning, impossible oaf. A west Waterfordman gave me this gloss: 'He's some rowdlamaun. He was asked by his boss if he could change the oil in his Mercedes, and could you credit what he did? He took the whole bloody engine apart, and now he can't put it together again!'

**Railimín**, sent to me as **ralameen** from many places in the west, is a weakling. 'How could they play that ralameen of a man at full back!' complained one of my informants. Another said he heard 'How much do you want for that ralameen of a pony?' at the famous Ballinasloe, Co. Galway, fair.

**Railiúnach** was rendered **rallianach** by Seumus MacManus, the Donegal writer, in *Bold Blades of Donegal* (1937). It means a loutish man. 'Pat's a rallianach of a fellow; too hasty in temper.'

**Ránaí** In Monaghan, Sligo, Westmeath and Dublin, **ránaí**, an Irish word for a thin, gaunt person or animal, has been rendered **rawnyeh** and **rawny**. A Sligo friend spoke of 'a little rawnyeh of a cat'. Joyce has **rawny** in *Finnegans Wake*; and I've heard the word myself in south-west Dublin county. There is another meaning. Two good friends of mine, the late Augustine Martin, professor of English at the National University of Ireland, Dublin, and John Mahon, both from Co. Leitrim, told me that a *rawny* was an imbecile.

**Rásaí** is well known in Co. Dublin in its Anglo-Irish forms, **rossie** and **raucie**. I have received in my time the following definitions. 'A rossie is a girl with a certain reputation, not a prostitute, but fond of it.' That was from a man who lives in the Liberties of Dublin city. 'A rossie is a rambling woman, a Gypsy woman', a woman from Shankill, in south Co. Dublin informed me. Paddy O'Neill, the collector of words from north Co. Dublin, said that 'a raucie is a gad-about girl.' James Joyce used the word in both *Ulysses* and *Finnegans Wake*. 'If they could run like rossies she could sit …' is from *Ulysses*. *Rás* is the Irish for a run, a race. *Rásaí* is, literally, a runner.

**Rawnsha** You might be given **rawnsha** at an *áirneán* (q.v.) in Co. Wexford. This is a word given to me by the late Elizabeth Jeffries, a storyteller and chanteuse from Kilmore, in the south of the county. 'My mother used to make the nicest rawnsha – rye bread, don't you know,' she told me. *Rawnsha* is an Irish compound heavily disguised – **arán seagail**; *seagal* (pronounced *shagul*) is rye. I must confess that I never found it very palatable.

**Rúcán** A Kilkenny **rúcán**, rendered **roocaun**, is, according to that great authority on Waterford Irish and Waterford and Kilkenny English, the late Dr R.B. Breathnach, 'a big rough man'. 'There was time', said a Slieverue, Co. Kilkennyman to him, 'when all they let into the police were big ignorant roocauns.' The Monaghan word **rúisceán**, rendered **rooishcaun**, 'a clumsy fellow', is a related word.

**Scalteen** Who nowadays makes a consommé as good as the traditional Irish **scailtín**, found in the literature as **scalteen**? *Scailtín* comes from the Irish *scalladh*, to scald. The German Prince with the fairy-tale name, Hermann Heinrich Ludwig von Pückler-Muskau, sampled scalteen after a hunt in Co. Tipperary back in Dan O'Connell's time. He was surprised to find that this soup was served between courses, and he came to the conclusion that it was meant to sober people up. It had quite the opposite effect on him. Fr Mathew, the temperance agitator, condemned the beverage in no uncertain terms, as did his friend, MacNamara Downes from Clare, a very bad temperance poet who formed the rather unsuccessful *Irish Water Drinkers Association*.

This heady soup was mentioned also in George A. Little's *Malachy Horan Remembers* (1943). Said old Malachy: 'They always had scalteen ready at Jobstown Inn. Men, in weather like this, out from morning till night without a bit, would be coming in with the mark of the mountain on them. Scalteen would make a corpse walk. It would put the life back into them, but make them drunk too. It was taken red hot. They made it from half a pint of whiskey, half a pound of butter, and six eggs.

You should try it some time, but when you have it down, go to bed while you are still able.' Old Malachy seems to have forgotten the main ingredient, the beef consommé.

I once asked the readers of my *Irish Times* Saturday column on words to send me any old recipe they might have been given for scalteen. This came from a man who signed his letter Mary Willie, the name of an old Tipperary pub much frequented by hurlers and hurling followers. Here is his recipe: 'Add half a bottle of whiskey, two whisked eggs, a lump of butter, to a pint and a half of unsalted and strained beef broth to which black pepper has been added. Heat the mixture but do not let it boil. Consume.' You have been warned.

**Sí** The **Sí**, spelled **shee** in Anglo-Irish literature, were the fairy host; the people of the *sí* or fairy mound. One rarely saw them, but their presence could be felt. The **sí gaoithe**, or **shee gwee** as the name was spelled in Co. Wexford, literally fairies of the wind, was a whirlwind, thought to be caused by fairies on the move.

**Slíbhín** A very common word in the Irish countryside is **slíbhín**, or **sleeveen**. It means a sly person. Flann O'Brien has the word in *The Dalkey Archive* (1976): 'What are you doing hiding there, you long-faced sleeveen?' Samuel Lover in *Legends and Stories of Ireland*, published in 1848, spells the word **sleeven**; one of his characters refers to 'a man being chated by a sleeven vagabond'. The word is onomatopoeic, I'd say.

**Trisk** This is one of the words sent to me from Co. Waterford recently; it is a seaweed. This is from the Irish **trioscar**, according to Dinneen's dictionary. Moylan has it in *The Language of Kilkenny*, from the estuary of the river Suir: 'seaweed growing on submerged rocks'. I am reminded of my friend Aidan Mathews' poignant poem *The Death of Irish*: 'The tide gone out for good,/ Thirty-one words for seaweed/ Whiten on the foreshore.' Well, *trisk* is one that has survived by being assimilated into the English of south-east Ireland.

**Yorks** (always plural) is an interesting word. They are bands of twisted straw or hay that farmers and farm labourers sometimes tie around their trousers below the knee; their purpose being to act as a kind of garter to keep the trouser-end up and free of mud. You'll find the word in many of the little glossaries of the English of Ireland put together in the nineteenth century. There is no trace of the word in Joseph Wright's great six-volume *English Dialect Dictionary*, finished around 1906; it is not in the standard dictionaries either. I am pretty sure that *yorks* is an Anglo-Irish form of the Irish **iarrach**, a binding.

SECTION TWO

# ULSTER ENGLISH

Contrary to what some 'experts' in the
European Union may think, Ulster Scots is
alive and well and living in parts of Down, Antrim
and east Donegal. It reached Ulster two years after
O'Neill and O'Donnell took flight to Rome and to
Spain in 1607. James I planted the lands they had
abandoned with, it is estimated, about 150,000
Scots settlers and about 20,000 English. It should
be remembered that the two forms of English
introduced into Ulster at the time of the
Plantation, the English of England and the English
of Scotland, had almost reached the stage of being
separate languages by then, rather as Swedish and
Danish separated in Scandinavia. It wasn't until the
time of the unification of both countries in the
eighteenth century that the English of London
became the standard in Scotland, though the Scots
spoke it with a Scots accent.

The language of the descendants of the Scots
planters in Ulster is often confused with the far
more widespread northern Hiberno-English, which
had its origin in a fusion of Irish, the English of
the English planters, and Scots. The situation is
less complicated in the south, where Hiberno-
English has a single origin in the English of
England, fused with Irish.

Ulster Scots, its speakers will tell you with pride, is 'purer', by which they mean more archaic, than the language now spoken in Scotland itself. The best introduction I can give you is a transcript of a recording made by my friend the late Brendan Adams, one of the foremost scholars in this field, back in the 1960s. You must imagine three old fellows having a chat in a farmhouse near Culleybackey in west Antrim. Their conversation ran like this; the explanations in parenthesis are mine:

'Jammie, you're an oul baachelor, A hear. It's a wundher ye naver merried.'

'Oh, you're aa wrang there, Joahn, A'm no an oul baachelor, A'm a weeda-maan. Aye, ma wife deed wheen we were jist a year merried, wheen harr waen (*child*) was boarn.'

'Weel, Jammie, A'm soary tae hear thaat, but it's a wundher ye navver merried again.'

'Weel, A had ma ee on Taam Sampson's doghter, Eggie, yannst (*once*) … Weel, efter thankin it ower a wheen a years (*many years*) A made it up wae Raab – ma croanyie sattin ower there on the haab (*hob*) – tae go an aaks her fether (*father*). A was gey (*good, very*) and scarred (*scared*), for Taam was doatin aboot laan (*land*), an me wae ma wee saiven acres wasnae very much tae waste a doghter on. Onyway, Raab here thought thaat it would be betther tae saafen Taam wae a dhraap o whusky – ye know Raab likes tae get saafened thaat wae hassel (*himself*). Weel, yan (*one*) Seturday naght A caad (*called*) for Raab tae go wae me – an A daddnae forget the whusky – but wheen A caad a coo (*cow*) was caavin, so he toul me tae go on. He was laanger ann (*in*) the leg nor me and he wud owertaak me. Wheen aai got ower thaon bautom o yours and throo the whuns (*whins*), A made for the slaap (*a gap in a fence*) whaur the kaay (*cows*) staans waitin tae be broght ann tae be malked. The next thang A knowed ma yann (*one*) fit (*foot*) slapped ann behann the ather yann an doon A went aan ma groof (*belly*) aan the coo shairn (*shit*). That wasnae aa. Wheen A spraaghled (*sprawled*) aboot trayin tae get up shae (*shoe*) nor fit cud a put undher me. A haad staived (*sprained*) me aankle. At laast A gaut on ma baakside an airsed (*arsed*) ower tae A gaut a houl o yann o thaun pailin posts fornint (*opposite, near*) the laant (*flax*) daam. A was there aboot an oor an A was chaakin wae the coul, an claarriet (*dirtied*) wae coo dung fae heel tae thraaple (*throat*). A thoght Raab wud navver come. At laast A hard his wheeple (*whistle*) ann the whuns, an A was gey an gled tae see his bagg feet as he lept ower the dike. He jist lucked at me an he says:

'Jammie, is thaat you?' Sez aai:

'"Whaa dae ye thank it wud be? A hae broke ma leg."

'"Naw!", sez he, "Is the whusky aa raght?"

Then he gaut his airse agann the stump o a tree an pulled oot his pipe. He laghtit a maatch. It blowed oot. Then he laghtit anather yann an hel it ower naxt maay face.

'"Jammie", sez he, "there's mair coo dung ann yer ear than wud grou (*grow*) a gid taap o praetas (*potatoes*)." A was gey an aangry at him. Wheen he smoked a while he says: "Kin ye maak the lenth o Taam's?"

'"A caan naut", sez aai, "A waant tae get away baak hame."

'At last Raab got me auxtered (*oxtered, helped by placing a shoulder under the other's armpit*) tae thon stile o' yours an we sut doon on it an drunk the whusky. Mine ye, A was quare an gled tae get anntae ma settle bed thaah naght.'

'Thaat was terrible, Jammie. But whut aboot Eggie? Dadd ye no go baak again aboot harr?'

'Naw, 'deed, Joahn, A navver bauthered.'

Very often in Ulster you'll find words of Scots origin enriching the speech of people who live in, or close to, the Gaelic-speaking areas. One may account for this by pointing out that Gaeltacht people had to emigrate in their thousands to Scotland, returning every summer to holiday at home; generations of them had also gone on seasonal migration as *tatie-hokers* (potato pickers); or working on the railroads, or excavating tunnels; or slaving in fish-processing plants.

You'll find words of Scots Gaelic origin in parts of Down and Antrim, and in east Donegal. This is because some of the Scots planters came from the Gaelic-speaking Highlands, and from western Galloway, which was, at the time of the Plantation, bilingual.

Here are some interesting words from the various Ulster Englishes.

**Aizins** An Antrim neighbour of mine pointed out to me recently that my aizins needed attention. **Aizins**, in places **easings**, are Ulster words for eaves. I found my friend's word in Hume's *Dialect of Down* (1890), and in W.J. Knowles's *Ballymena Observer* (1892), a treasury of Ulster words and phrases. It is good to see that the northerners, so conservative in their language, have preserved the old word. It is common still in Scotland and in

northern England. Its origin is the older *eavesing*,
representing Old English *efesung*, a verbal noun.
Langland's *Piers Plowman*, which is from the
fourteenth century, has 'As we may seo a wynter,
isykles in euesynges.'

**Beekin** The act of sunbathing, and the act of
lounging in front of a fire, is known in Ulster as
**beekin**. You'll find this verb in both Scots and
English literature. In a polemic entitled *Vindication
of Charles I*, written in 1648, its author solemnly
informs us that 'That Pope of Rome, when he lay
beakin himself in the midst of his luxuries, had
cause to cry.' 'She and her cat sit beekin in her
yard,' sang the influential Scots poet Ramsay, in
1725. Long before that, in or about 1400, the
author of *Ywaine* complained about a knight that
'ligges beakand in his bed, When he haves a lady
wed.' What else did he expect him to do? **To beek**
also meant to heat wood at a fire in order to make
it more pliable. It was done by ships' carpenters in
the old days and is still done by Antrim
basketmakers. As to origin, here we have a classic
example of the dangers of jumping to conclusions
in matters of etymology. Obviously related to *bake*
(from Old English *bacan*, or Old Norse *baka*) you
might think; but as the Oxford Dictionary points
out, an Old Teutonic *bekian*, from *bok*, past tense
of *bakan*, would have given Old English *bóecen* or
*bécan*, and Middle English *beke* or *beek*, but no

trace of the older forms exists. So, the origin of the Ulster *beekin* is uncertain.

**Blithe-meat** is a compound used by William Carleton in *Fardorougha the Miser*. It was the meal prepared for visitors at the birth of a child. I was delighted to find the word in C.I. Macafee's *Concise Ulster Dictionary*, because this points to its survival in the province. She also gives the word a second meaning: a gathering of friends to celebrate the birth of a child. Carleton wrote: 'After having kissed and admired the babe … they set themselves to the distribution of the blythe (sic) meat …' The word appears again in word lists from Armagh and Donegal sent to Joseph Wright, who was then (1880) engaged in assembling his monumental *English Dialect Dictionary* at Oxford. **Blithe-meat** is not confined to Ireland. It has been recorded in Ayr and Galloway; and in Shetland and Orkney as *blyd-meat*. I don't know what the meal consisted of in Ulster, but in Galloway they usually served a special cheese called *cryin-oot cheese*. *Blithe* is a Common Teutonic word which appears in Old English as *blithe*, and in Old Norse as *blithr*, mild. The Oxford Dictionary says that the earliest application was to the outward expression of kindly feeling, sympathy, affection to others. *Meat* was pronounced *mate*, of course, the older form in both Scots and English.

**Bye-name** Still used in parts of Co. Down for a nickname, or a name other than the one registered at baptism or marriage. The word is also in use across the water in Scotland, Cumbria, Northumberland, Durham and north Yorkshire. It is an old word. Holland's *Plutarch's Morals* of 1603 has: 'He got himself a by-name, and everie man called him Epaminindas.' As far as Co. Down is concerned, we may assume that the word came there with the Scots planters. Sir Walter Scott was fond of the word; it turns up time and time again in his novels. 'The inferior sort o' people, ye'll observe, are kent by sorts o' bye-names, some o' them, as Glaiket Christie and the Dewke's Gibbie,' he wrote in *Guy Mannering*.

Bye-names are common all over Ireland. The late lexicographer Tomás de Bhaldraithe once told me of being asked by the courts to help solve a problem which had arisen over claims to lands in west Cork. Everybody seemed to be Greenes and Whites in the place concerned, and yet the land was registered to nobody but O'Sullivans in the nineteenth century. The explanation was that to distinguish between the two local O'Sullivan clans, Ó Súilleabháin Glas and Ó Súilleabháin Bán, the former were known only by their bye-name *Glas*, which the National Schools translated as *Greene*, and the latter by the bye-name *Bán*, turned into *White* by schoolmasters, and afterwards by solicitors.

**Clash** A child's word heard all over the north is *clash*, a verb which means to tell tales out of school, to give the game away on another. Here again we have a Scots word, and it is also in the dialects of Northern English as a noun meaning gossip, tittle-tattle, scandal. *Clash*, a tale bearer, is common in Ulster speech. Burns has 'Some rhyme to court the countra clash' in his poem *To James Smith*. The phrase **to carry clashes** is still common in the schoolyards of both Scotland and Ulster.

**Convenient** I wonder is the word **convenient**, meaning near, adjacent to, used much outside Ulster any more, where you'll still hear the likes of 'I lived convenient to him when I was young' and 'It was convenient to five o'clock when I got home'? It was common enough in 'genteel' speech in the south-east when I grew up, but I haven't heard anybody use it in years. This particular use of *convenient* is, apparently, peculiar to Ireland. The *English Dialect Dictionary* could find no trace of it across the water, and that great work spread its net far and wide. It is from the Latin *convenientem*, present participle of *convenire*, to come together, meet, unite etc; there was also a French *convenient* recorded in the twelfth century, from the same source. I am tempted to speculate that our unique *convenient* was a product of the hedge schools, whose teachers often knew more Latin than English.

**Convoy** I often receive letters asking about the Donegal verb **convoy**, a word used there with the special meaning 'to see somebody home'. I am usually asked, even by Donegal people, if the word is a Donegal 'mistake' for *convey*? It is not. It is an import from Scotland. Rab Burns in *The Cotter's Saturday Night* has, 'To do some errands and convoy her home'. It came into Scots from the Old Central French *convoier*, which has a counterpart in Italian *conviare*. Is it related to *convey*? The answer is no. Look at it this way. Although *convoier* was adapted into English and Scots as *convoy*, the latter word was 'corrected' in Renaissance English as *conveigh*, implying a mistaken notion of derivation from Latin *convehere*, to carry; *convey* is simply not related to this word.

**Craig** A long time ago in a doctor's surgery in Co. Donegal, I struck up a conversaton with a young man of about six who happened to be suffering from the same ailment as myself, a badly infected throat. When I asked him what was wrong with him he told me that he had a sore craig; his mother, I remember, had to interpret for me. Another old Scots word this. Robert Burns wrote of 'the knife that nicket Abel's craig' in *Captain Grose's Perigrinations*. A century later Robert Louis Stevenson has 'A rope to your craig and a gibbet to clatter your bones on', in *Catriona*. The Scots have some interesting compounds not found in Ulster as far as I know: *craig-bane*, collarbone; *craig-cloth*, a tie, a cravat; *craig o' mutton*, the lean part of a neck of mutton, also called **scrag**. *Craig* is old. The poet Dunbar has it in *Flyting* (1505): 'Thy lang lean craig. Thy pure pynnit (*dry or shrunk*) thrott.' It is from the Middle Dutch *craegh*, the neck.

**Distasted** This old word survives in Fermanagh and in Antrim. It is used to describe food gone off, spoiled. Here, surely, we have a survivor from the days of the first English settlers in Ulster. You'll find this word in Shakespeare's *Troilus and Cressida*. In one of the most beautiful passages in literature, Troilus complains with heart-stopping poignancy of the hurried leave-taking that has been forced upon himself and Cressida … 'And scants us with a single famish'd kiss/ Distasted with the salt of broken tears.'

**Douce** is a lovely adjective from Ulster. 'She keeps a douce house,' said a friend to me recently; she was complimenting an elderly Donegal neighbour for keeping her house neat and tidy and very comfortable. *Douce* can also mean gentle, kindly and sweet-tempered in Down and Antrim, so the invaluable *Ballymena Observer* (1892) tells me. It also says that the adjective is generally applied to elderly housekeepers. Because of their tidiness, or their kindliness? you might ask. From

the latter, I'd say, because the word, also found in
Scotland and in northern England, is from Middle
English *douce*, or *dowce*, from Old French *dous*,
later *doux* (feminine *douce*), ultimately from the
Latin *dulcis*, sweet.

**Draghy** I'm sure that most of us have travelled
**draghy roads** in our time – roads that are deceptive
in the sense that they are longer than they appear
to be. I know one in Donegal between Muckish
mountain, whose name may have something do
with *muc*, pig, and the lovely cone of Errigal,
which was named from some hermit's *oraculum*, or
place of prayer. I once walked this road, cut from
the loveliest scenery in Ireland, and I thought it
would never end. 'It's a draghy road, all right,' said
a man in a pub to me, when I reached Dunlewey,
at its end, at last. Michael Traynor's *The English
Dialect of Donegal*, published in 1955, has the
compound. Traynor thought that it was a
translation of the Irish *bealach draíochta*, magic (i.e.
deceptive) road or way. That seems a bit fanciful to
me. I am inclined to think that **draghy** is a variant
of **drawky**, a Scots adjective which means dull,
dreary, murky. It is associated with damp, misty
weather, and its ultimate origin is Scandinavian.
Compare the Old Norse *drakkja*, to submerge.

**Dwaum** is an old word you won't find in the
southern counties of Ireland. It means a swoon or a

fit of weakness, and you might fall in a dwaum from working too hard. You might also experience a dwaum from having taken a drop too much; in that context I myself heard the word used in Donegal. The old nineteenth-century glossaries, such as Simmons's from south Donegal and W.H. Patterson's from Down and Antrim, and some new ones too, have the word. It has a Teutonic origin. Old Saxon, for example, has *dwalm* for delusion, and Old English has *dwolma* for chaos. No doubt the word came to Ulster with the Scots planters. The Scots poet Dunbar has 'Sic deidlie dwaalmes' in a poem written around 1510, and the word is still in vogue in many parts of 'the land beyond the stream of Moyle', as the ancient Irish called Scotland, 'an tír thar Sruth na Maoile'.

**Farra** A few years ago I got a letter from a lady who said that when her Tyrone mother came to visit her they discussed plans for an extension to her (my correspondent's) home. The older woman thought that this was a waste of money, and suggested that her daughter convert the farra instead. By *farra* she meant the attic. In the older Ulster houses the *farra* or **farry** was a half-loft. In houses which didn't have this loft, the roof space above the ceiling was called the farra (or farry), and was used as a storage space. This much the *Concise Ulster Dictionary* tells me. These words are from the Irish **faradh**, a loft, according to Fr Dinneen's dictionary. It has another meaning, a roost for hens, he tells us. I have never come across the word *faradh* for a loft in the Donegal Gaeltacht, and their word for a hen roost is **aradh**. Mysterious, how the word changed its meaning in Tyrone-among-the-bushes.

**Flipe** Michael Traynor's 1955 *The English Dialect of Donegal* is a worthy book, written, believe it or not, in Tasmania, with no e-mails and no fax machines to speed his progress. He was blessed in his contributors back home, for all that; one of the words sent to him was one I've heard time and again beyond Muckish mountain – **flipe**. This comes directly from the Scots, where it has an identical meaning: an impudent, flirtatious girl. Bernard Share quotes from *Our Son*, part of *Livin' in Drumlister*, that Ulster classic by W.F. Marshall: 'An the wee back room it wud never do/ For the flipe that was raired in the South.' William Carleton, too, was fond of the word. 'Who made you my misthress, you blaggard flipe?' asks a nice gent in *Fardorougha the Miser*. In Scotland *flipe* was sometimes used in a contemptuous sense of a man; in Ulster it was, and is, used only to insult women. The original meaning of *flipe* was a forehead-cloth worn by women. It is of Scandinavian origin. Danish had *flip*, a protruding piece of shirt, kerchief, etc. In 1530 the important lexicographer Palsgrave has 'I tourne up the flepe of a cap.' It seems that the fashionable *flipes*, then considered saucy and sexy, gave *flipes*, the women who wore them. This type of transference is common in many languages. Consider the French *garnement*, defined as (1) *garniture d'habit* and (2) *mauvais sujet*, a bad lot, a ne'er-do-well, by the lexicographer La Curne.

**Fosey** This word, sometimes spelled **fozy**, is used in Co. Armagh, and in various places in Antrim and Down as well, to describe very fresh bread. It is referred to in many of the old Ulster glossaries; one of them glosses it as 'light, spongy, soft'. In the Ulster countryside it is often used of vegetables, turnips in particular. The word probably came to Ulster from Scots but it is common in England's North Country, and is found as far south as East Anglia.

In Scotland the word has also come to mean fat, bloated. 'Gin I hed been a dizzen o' year younger, I wud a' tann't the muckle fozy hide o' ye', wrote Alexander in his engaging *Ain Folk* in 1862. The word has also come to mean stupid, dull-witted. I heard a man from Fanad, Co. Donegal so describe a local footballer who had missed an open goal.

**Foundered** 'How are you?' said I to a Derryman of my acquaintance. It was a cold day, and he replied, 'I'm foundered. How about a drop of whiskey to put the life back in me?' *Foundered* to him meant very cold. A funny old word this, with many meanings in Ireland. For example, I once asked a Wicklowman to have a pint with me and he refused, explaining that he had been at the races all day and he was foundered. In this instance foundered meant full to the gills, drunk. In Wexford, Carlow, Kilkenny and south Tipperary foundered means exhausted, prostrate with fatigue.

The word has another meaning. Used of horses it means lame. I've heard Travellers who deal in horses talk of various cures for foundered horses. I was told by the keeper of the word-hoard of Monaghan and Cavan, Peadar Ó Casaide, that this usage was, in his youth, very common. W.H. Patterson recorded it in his Down and Antrim glossary of 1880. Jonathan Swift once wrote of galloping a foundered horse up a causeway. Long before him Geoffrey Chaucer, in *The Knight's Tale*, mentioned that 'his hors for feer gan to turne and leep asyde and foundred as he leep.' Foundered in all its shades of meaning is from the Old French *fondrer*, to submerge, to collapse. *Fondrer* is rare in Old French, but is common in the compounds *esfondrer* and *enfondrer* that have a variety of meanings, such as to burst, smash; of a boat, to fill with water and sink; of a building, to fall down. The origin of the French words is the Latin *fundus*, bottom.

**Friend** Any lexicographer dealing with regional dialects depends on erudite correspondents. One of my most reliable was the scholarly Peadar Ó Casaide from Monaghan, mentioned above. His last list contained the word **friend**, which, he explained, did not mean a pal, but a relative by blood or marriage. *The English Dialect Dictionary*, I found, has 'We are near friends, but we don't speak', from Co. Cavan. W.H. Patterson's Down and Antrim glossary from the late nineteenth century, has the sentence 'They are far-out friends of mine but I niver seen 'em.' This usage is also found in Scotland and in Northumberland. Common Teutonic, the Old English is *fréond*, the Old Icelandic *fraend*, the Old High German *friunt*. The northern Irish sense is the only sense of the word found in the Scandinavian languages, where the sense 'pal' is expressed by the Old Norse *vinr*, and by the Modern Danish *ven*. In many High German dialects, too, *freund* means kinsman. Compare the Old Icelandic *fraend-kona*, a kinswoman, and *freendlauss*, kinless. Shakespeare used 'friend' in this sense in *The Two Gentlemen of Verona*: 'She is promised by her friends unto a youthful gentleman of worth.' This sense was brought to Ulster by the English planters, you may bet your life on it.

**Frou** is in general dialect use in Ulster and is not found elsewhere in the country. Across the water it is confined to Scotland and northern England. It means a big, fat, untidy, coarse woman; also a woman of low character in Scotland. Sometimes

spelled **frow**, the word was in English in 1390.
A will made in that year refers to 'Margareta
Quellyngbourgh Frowe'. No sign of disparagement
here. The origin of the word is the Dutch *vrouw*, a
woman, a wife, cognate, of course with the
German *Frau*; and for centuries after Margareta's
time a **frow** was simply a woman of Dutch birth,
assumed by the English, because she usually had
money, to be a lady. It was not until the eighteenth
century that *frow*, meaning a slut, emerged. The
editor of the *Concise Ulster Dictionary* has not
found this meaning in Ulster.

**Fud** is a word I've heard only in the north of
Ireland, and it has given the etymologists a lot to
think about. It means the tail or scut of a rabbit, but
its use is extended: a footballer is laughed at for
falling on his fud, and you may hear cornerboys
praise the shape of a passing female fud. It is
common in Scotland and is in general dialect use in
England, I see. Burns has '[they] pawned their duds/
they scarcely left to co'er their fuds' in *The Jolly
Beggars*. It is, I think, of Scandinavian origin. The
Old Norse has *futh*, an obscene word for the vulva.
*Futh* has been formally identified with the Sanskrit
*putau*, buttocks, so, in one form or another, it has
been around for a very long time indeed.

**Fushion** This was one of my late wife's words.
Her father was from the Irish-speaking parish of

Gweedore, her mother from the neighbouring district of the Rosses, and she herself was born in Glasgow. She would say: 'There's great fushion in porridge' or 'There's no fushion in that food.' *Fushion* means nourishment. You'll hear the word in Antrim, and that great source of Ulster words, *The Ballymena Observer* (1892), also has **fushionless**: 'Applied to meal or flour which has been damaged; insipid or innutritious, as applied to fodder of inferior quality.' The word has many variant spellings across the water, *foison*, *fuzzen* and *fusen* among them. Scots the word is, but the auld alliance with France pointed towards a French origin; Randle Cotgrave's French-English dictionary of 1611 solved the problem: it defined the French *foison* as 'store, plenty, abundance'. May I tip my cap, too, towards Worlidge's *Dictionarium Rusticum* of 1681 which gave me, as a definition of the variant *fusen*, 'nourishment, natural juyce'.

**Gillery**, deception, fraud, trickery, is a word you'll hear in parts of Down and Antrim. You might expect that here we have a Scots word, the legacy of the planters, but no. There's not a trace of the word in the Scots dictionaries. The *English Dialect Dictionary*, which has the word from Antrim, says that it is also found in England's North Country, south to Nottinghamshire and Lincolnshire. The *Lincoln Chronicle*, writing about the football hooligans of 1888, says that the game was 'mixed up with the greatest gillery, roguery and blackguardism'. *Gilery* is found in the *York Plays* of c. 1400. It is from the Old French *gillerie*, trickery, from *guiler*, to beguile, deceive, and thus it is related to the modern English *guile*.

**Glar** is Ulster mud; Seamus Heaney also has it in its adjectival form **glarry**. The Donegal Irish form is *glár*, but that is a borrowing. From where? From Scots, certainly, but further back? We can only guess. Perhaps, as the Oxford Dictionary suggests tentatively, from Old Norse *leir*, mud.

**Grunts** In the first poem of his collection *Electric Light* Seamus Heaney calls the fish, perch, **grunts**. This northern word, mentioned in the old Ulster dialect dictionaries, is a bit of a mystery. How it came to Ulster, and from where, nobody knows. It is not in any of the dialect dictionaries, Scots or English, to my knowledge, but another poet knew of it. Elizabeth Barrett Browning, in her 1851 *Casa Guidi Windows*, has: 'The pool in front/ Where in the hill stream trout are cast to wait/ The beatific vision, and the grunt/ Used at refectory, keeps its weedy state …'

**Hooghmagandie** I can see how an elder of a severe kirk would see in *horbgorbling* (q.v.) a stage on the road to perdition and to what Robert Burns called *houghmagandie*. This marvellous, fanciful formation for fornication may be from the noun

**hough**, in Scotland and in Ulster the back part of the thigh, plus the adjective **canty**, gleesome, lively. Of the *Holy Fair* Rhymer Rab wrote memorably: 'There's some are fou (*full*) o' love divine/ And some are fou o' brandy,/ And monie jobs that day begin/ May end in houghmagandie …' This wonderful word has, like *horbgorblin'*, reached Ulster, I'm glad to say, and can be heard in Antrim and Down.

**Horbgorble** This word was sent to me not long ago by a Co. Antrim correspondent. It crossed the Moyle from Scotland; when, we don't know. It travelled to the United States in the eighteenth century, where it survives to the present day. Given the great Presbyterian exodus from Ulster in that century, it may well have reached the New World from this country, and not from Scotland. A friend of mine from Philadelphia sent me a newspaper-cutting just after the last presidential election, and it bemoaned the fact that Mr Gore hadn't the sense to use the undoubted charisma of Mr Clinton to gain more votes. 'Gore spent his time horbgorbling around,' the writer claimed, meaning that he travelled about in a feckless manner, fumbling, or mooching, as we say in Ireland.

The late Ivor Brown, Scottish journalist and lexicographer, once wrote about the trial of a young Caithnessman for alleged sexual assault on a servant girl. It was a strange business. The case was brought, not by the girl, but by her employer, who was, he felt, *in loco parentis*. There was no suggestion of rape, but there was a suggestion of sexual misdemeanour, even though the girl was over the age of consent; so the magistrates asked her what exactly had happened. The lass explained that her boyfriend was only horbgorblin' when the employer came on the scene. This explanation was readily accepted by the court. The employer was told that he was a meddling auld fool and the case was dismissed.

**Lock** All over Ulster you will hear the word *lock*. Farmers will tell you in public houses on fair days that they have to go outside to give their cattle or sheep a lock of hay; you'll hear shopkeepers tell of having a nice lock of spuds or cabbage just delivered to them. The word seems to be confined nowadays to the north, although there is some evidence, in the writings of the Kilkenny Banim brothers, and in the novels of Lever and Lover, that the word was once used in the southern half of the country. I myself have never heard it south of Cavan and Monaghan. The Ulster *lock* is an enigma. It may be from Scots, but it may also be another survivor from the English of the 1609 Plantation. Still common all over Scotland, it survives, too, from the Scottish border right down to Dorset, Devon and Cornwall. The earliest quotation in literature is from a c. 1440 English

glossary in which a 'lok of hey or other lyke' is
mentioned. Gascoigne's charming *Posies* of 1575
has 'Fewe men wyll lend a locke of heye, but for to
gaine a loade.' Nearer to our own time, Thomas
Hardy has 'Curl up and sleep in a lock of straw' in
*Far From The Madding Crowd*. So, where did this
one come from? It is Teutonic, that's for sure. The
Old English is *loc*; the Middle Dutch *locke*. And
consider the Old Norse *lokkr*, the same word as we
have in 'a lock of hair'.

**Midden** Ask any Ulster farmer and he'll tell you
that a dung heap is a *midden*. You won't hear this
word in the other three provinces. It is an import
from Scotland, but you'll find it in many places in
England, a fact that may point you to its ultimate
origin in Viking territory. Ferguson's Scottish
*Proverbs* of 1641 tells us that 'a cock is crouse
(brave) on his own midding'. Not so long ago
farmers in all parts were proud of the size of their
middens, and it was common to see them in full
view of the front door, in all parts of this country.
All advice about the dangers of this practice was
ignored. W.G. Lyttle, his tongue in his cheek, had
this to say about the matter in *Life in Ballycuddy,
Co. Down*, published over a century ago: 'We hae
been readin' in the newspapers aboot them
middens. A beleeve a weel-biggit (*well built*)
midden is a sonsy (*pleasant looking*), wholesome
thing aboot ony man's hoose, an' guid fur the

appetite.' Lest you think that this particular disdain of agricultural hygiene was confined to this country, *The English Dialect Dictionary* quotes an old Northumbrian quatrain, of which there are many Irish varieties: 'Berwick is a dirty town/ A church without a steeple,/ There's a midden at every door;/ God curse all the people.' As to the word's origin, it is from the Old Norse *myki-dyngia*. The first element means dung; the second, heap, especially a heap of dung, according to Vigfusson's dictionary. Incidentally, *myki* also gave us the word *muck*.

**Pree** This verb means taste in Ulster. It is a contracted form of *prieve*. This, too, is Scots. 'The proof of the pudding is in the preeing of it', is a Donegal version of the saying.

*To pree* also means to kiss in Scots, and this, too, I heard in Donegal. 'Aye he preed her cherry mou,' wrote the great Hogg long ago. From Old French *prover*, from Latin *probare*, to test as to goodness.

**Rig** The word has many meanings but I feel sure that the one sent to me by an old salt who fished out of Killybegs, in Donegal, is not one to spring to the lips of anybody but old-timers from the fishing ports. The man who sent it to me lamented the fact that many of the old weather words may have gone out of use since his time, including this one, which means a fierce gust of wind. I was heartened to hear it used by a man from the

opposite end of the country, Carne, Co. Wexford –
Phil Wall, another ancient mariner who has since
died. The word is related to the Old Icelandic
*hregg*, storm and rain.

**Silly** I've heard **silly** used in the senses pliable,
limp, poor in health, helpless, in east Donegal.
A fishing rod, or sallies used in weaving baskets,
could be said to be silly. Not long ago I heard a
Donegal chef complain from his kitchen that the
lettuce had gone silly. A table cloth could be silly
from want of starch. Robert Burns liked the word.
Sir Walter Scott has 'Your health seems but silly' in
*The Heart of Midlothian*. From c. 1550 to c. 1675,
according to the Oxford Dictionary, *silly* was used
extensively in England in the above senses. It is a
later form of Middle English *syly*, defenceless,
weak, pitiable. Long may it live in Donegal.

**Skilly, skillygolee** Northern people still
use the word *skilly* for thin, watery porridge. It
comes from the fanciful formation *skillygolee*, still
in common use north of the border – a word
which started life in the British navy, the Oxford
Dictionary says. I once observed a Donegal sheep
farmer sending back a bowl of soup he had
ordered. Consommé was what the waitress brought
him; he had expected good Scotch broth. He told
her that he had a mind for aul' skillygolee.

The words *skilly* and *skillygolee* are also used to

describe weak tea or coffee. The earliest reference to *skillygolee* is in a memoir written by a sailor in 1819: 'Tolerable flour, of which the cook composes a certain flour for breakfast, known among sailors as skilygolee, being in plain English, paste.' From the ships it transferred to the workhouse, and later to the jail. In both places it was watery gruel. George Sala's *Gaslight and Daylight* (1858) has: 'In some Unions they give you bread and cheese, in some broth, and in some skillygolee.' John Masefield in *The Conway* (1933) has the transferred use of the word: 'A cup of skilly completed the repast.' He had weak tea in mind.

**Slabber** Re-reading Seamus Heaney's *The Midnight Verdict* recently I got to wondering about his good Ulster word **slabber**, verb and noun. We would use **slobber** in the south. Heaney's word means excessive talk, guff, blather. His couplet is: 'Their one recourse is the licensed robber/ With his legalese and his fancy slabber.' The primary meaning of *slabber*, verb, was to salivate excessively. In Yorkshire, to slabber meant to wet the thread with spit in the process of spinning. The word has a Dutch or German origin. Compare the Dutch *slabberen*, Low German *slabbern*, to befoul with saliva. The compound *beslabberen* is found in Middle English. The Irish **slabar** is a borrowing from the dialectal English.

**Sneck** is an Ulster word for the latch of a door. Its etymology is unknown, but it did come from either Scots or England's North Country. I can trace it back to the fifteenth century, but no further.

**Snib** I have seen these on many's the farmhouse kitchen door in Ulster. This is how one dialect dictionary describes it: 'The snib is a small piece of wood by inserting which into the loop, the sneck becomes fast and cannot be raised from the outside.' I've also heard the ordinary sliding bolt referred to as a snib in Donegal, and not long ago I heard a young woman remind her boyfriend to snib the car door after he had parked it outside a hotel in Dungloe. Common in Scotland, too. I suppose this word is related to *snib* meaning to check, restrain. If I'm right, the word has a Scandinavian origin. Compare the Middle Swedish *snybba*, which also meant to rebuke. This is what Chaucer had in mind when he wrote, 'Hym wold be snibben sharply for the nones.'

**Strone** is a word I've heard in Donegal. It was also sent to me by a woman who lives in the town of Antrim. She told me of her first day in school, and of her prissy teacher's feigned shock at her request to be allowed out to strone. To strone meant to pee; it was the noun as well. In Donegal *strone* is the stream of milk got from a cow at one pull. I was amazed to see that the major dialect dictionaries say that the word is of unknown origin. Surely it is, in the case of Donegal, from the Irish *sruthán*, or in the case of Antrim, from the Scots Gaelic *sruthan*, a stream.

**Throng** An honest Ulsterman came here to my house in Co. Wicklow the other day, inquiring as to whether I had any odd jobs to be done. He looked at my garden, in which noxious weeds had begun to rear their heads. He promised to return soon; he was too *throng*, he said, to start the job immediately, which led me to believe that gardening is not his forte either. I know I'll never see him again. I hadn't heard the word *throng* in a long while, although I've seen it in both Bernard Share's book *Slanguage* and in *The Concise Ulster Dictionary* recently. Used of a place it means crowded, very busy; of a person, busy, fully occupied. The Donegalman Seumus MacManus, in his engaging story *The Rocky Road To Dublin* (1938), has this: 'Because Billy had no help footering with his farm and wrestling with cattle, he had been "too throng" ever to go courting.' Another Ulster writer, Lynn Doyle, from the east of the province, has this in *Ballygullion* (1908): 'And the market day being a throng day for the polis in Ballygullion, it was ginerally Billy's throng day outside av it, delivering a wee keg here and there.'

It would seem from the evidence of literature that this word was once used in the south and west of Ireland, but if it still exists there I'm not aware of it. Somerville and Ross, the creators of the *Irish R.M.*, have 'We were as throng as three in a bed', in *Some Irish Yesterdays*. Lover has 'Mighty throng it wuz wid the boys and the girls', in his *Legends and Stories of Ireland* (1848). Its ultimate origin? The Scots form is *thrang*. You'll find *thrang* and *throng* in Middle English, probably shortened from Old English *gethrang*, crowd, tumult.

**Tidy** Aidan O'Hara, author and folklorist, sent me this Donegal word. **The cow is tidy** means that she is in calf. In Burns's country *a tidy bride* is 'one who goes home to her bridegroom's side in a state of pregnancy', according to the *English Dialect Dictionary*. I'm sure this never happens in Donegal. The origin of this tidy is the Middle English *tid*, time.

**Traikle** A Donegal correspondent gave me the word *traikle*, noun, a lazy person. She has a noun *traik*, a long, tiresome walk. *Traikle* is from *traik*, a verb, which has many shades of meaning. *To traik* in Scots and Donegal English means to walk about, to loaf, to wander, to get lost. 'He's none of your birds that traik' is a Donegal expression meaning that he won't be seen to do anything unconventional. *To traik* also means to walk slowly and with difficulty. From this they made **traikin**, to be unwell; and in the bad old days to be **traiked**

meant to have contracted tuberculosis. As to origin, more than one word may be involved here, as the *Concise Ulster Dictionary* observes. Consider the Norwegian dialectal *traka*, to labour at some difficult task, and the Dutch *trekken* to travel, the origin of *trek*, too, of course.

**Tried** Having had an interest in horses all my life, an interest that included owning and hunting a few, I am always glad to hear of local words for a horse's ailments. I was a sent a word from Monaghan a few years ago which interested me greatly. The word is *tried*, a noun. Here is an Irish word anglicised. The origin is Irish **treighid**, defined by Dinneen as 'a stitch, gripe, or colic; a pang, bitter grief'. He mentioned a specific for colic in a horse, the herb sage, *sáiste* in Irish. 'Cé gheobhaidh bás agus sáiste ar an gcnoc?' is an old saying meaning 'Why die when there's sage on the hill?' Sage advice, if you'll pardon the awful pun.

SECTION THREE

# HIBERNO-ENGLISH

The Cromwellian settlement of the 1650s removed native Irish landowners to the province of Connacht, and their confiscated estates in Leinster and Munster were taken over by English colonists, thus planting in the south of Ireland the English of England, in its many dialects and variations. In the course of time, mainly because there was very little travel between Ireland and England prior to the Act of Union of 1800, this Cromwellian English became more estranged from the language spoken across the Irish sea, a language which developed greatly in the years when the Cromwellian planter's English remained doggedly conservative, absorbing, at the same time, a vast number of Irish-based words and phrases.

Jonathan Swift supplies evidence for this. In his *A Dialogue in Hibernian Stile* and in *Irish Eloquence*, two burlesque pieces, he castigates the kind of English spoken in Ireland two generations after the Cromwellian incursion. Some sentences he found to be direct translations from the Irish, incomprehensible to people who lived across the water: *'Pray, how does he get his health?'* meaning 'How is his health?'; *'It is kind father for you'*, meaning 'You have been handed down that tendency by your father'; *'I wonder what is gone with them?'* meaning 'I wonder what has happened to them?' *'Lend me a loan of your last newspaper till I read it over'* still has a decidedly Irish ring about it.

Thomas Sheridan in his *Dictionary of the English Language*, published in 1780, lists 55 words whose pronunciation differed from English pronunciation; he is also amused by the Irishman's pronunciation of meat, sea, tea and please as *mate*, *say*, *tay* and *plase*, pronunciations still heard in places in rural Ireland, as is *psawm* and *cawm* for 'psalm' and 'calm' in parts of west Cork to this day.

The Irishman of the eighteenth century had no chance of learning standard English; modern Hiberno-English is all the richer for it. Here's a sampler:

---

**A** If you listen carefully to the speech of country people in Ireland you will hear echoes from the distant past. I was reminded of this fact by a letter from a Kilkenny schoolboy who was born and brought up in Surrey, and who is intrigued by the prefix **a** which he now hears continually around him. This *a* represents the Old English preposition *on*, and my young friend's examples are: '**He was here a Friday**' and '**His house went afire.**' This is not confined to the south-east; in Antrim I came across the adverb **alow**, which means 'on fire'. Here we have *a* on, and *low*, from the Old Norse *loge*, a flame, a blaze. The south-east Wexford adverb **amain**, strongly, at full speed, also contains *a*, but representing Old English *a-*, earlier *ar-*, originally implying motion onward, hence used as an intensive prefix. 'The work is going on amain, and the house will be roofed before the Christemas,' said an old Wexford fisherman, Jack Devereux of Kilmore Quay, to me once. *Main* is from the Old English *maegn*, force, power. 'Cry you all amain, Achilles hath the mighty Hector slain,' wrote Shakespeare in *Troilus and Cressida*.

Jane Barlow, a poor enough novelist who flourished at the end of the nineteenth century, but whose ear for dialect was acute, used *a* as a prefix of state or condition. Her *Bogland* is set in the west, and there she heard 'The air was a-fluther wid snow', and 'When th'ould master had tore it wid his hands all a-shake …' She used *a* with the verb *to be* to form continuous sense: 'I'm a-thinkin …' In Wexford and Kilkenny *a* is used for the preposition *with*: '**She's adin**', meaning within; **adout**, outside. This is general in dialects all over England, except that they pronounce the words *athin* and *athout*. Indeed, all the examples I have given above are still in use in England, as is the use of *a* as the indefinite article before numerals and nouns of multitude and quality. All over the south and west of Ireland I've heard such as 'There's not **a one** of today's hurlers who could hould a candle to Christy Ring or Mick Mackey.' This was said to me by a great Tipperary hurler of yesteryear, reminding me of Shakespeare's *Macbeth*: 'There's not a one of them but in his house I keep a servant fee'd,' and Chaucer's 'And up they rysen, wel a ten or twelve.' As I said, listen carefully and you'll hear the echoes from the past …

**Again** This dialect adverb, meaning 'in time for', is alive and well in Ireland, I'm glad to say. A Wicklow shoemaker told me the other day that he'd have my shoes mended 'again you come back'. The Elizabethan dramatist Philip Massenger in his play *City Madam* has: 'His cap and pantofles ready, and a candle again you rise' (*pantofles* is from French *pantoufle*, a slipper, by the way). A Waterford farmer's wife told me that she'd keep a bronze turkey for me 'again the Christmas'. Chaucer has the word in this sense: 'Ageyn this lusty somere's tyde/ This mirroure … He has sent.'

There is another sense recorded in Ireland, *again* meaning 'in the future'. I've heard 'Look, I haven't time to do it now, but I'll do it again', in south Carlow and in Wexford. The *English Dialect Dictionary* asks us to compare this usage with that found in the 1611 translation of Genesis: 'I will not again curse the ground any more for man's sake.'

**Alfraits** You'll find **alfraits** in both the Irish and the English of the south. He is a rough spoken man in west Cork; a scoundrel in Kerry. This is from the dialect English *fratch*, a testy person; *oul' fratch* becoming *alfraits*.

**Angry** is how my Wexford grandmother would describe a red, inflamed wound or sore. This adjective is common all over England. Shakespeare used it in *Othello*: 'I have rubb'd this young quat almost to the sense,/ And he grows angry', says Iago to Roderigo. (A *quat*, by the way, is a pimple. Its origin is unknown, and it is not in use in Ireland, as far as I know.) John Florio, one of my favourite lexicographers, has this definition of *pedignoni* in his Italian-English dictionary, *The Worlde of Wordes*, in 1598: 'angrie kibes, chillblains'. This *angry* is common in Irish speech, north and south of the border. It is from the Old Norse *angr*, grief; related to Old English *enge*, Old High German *engi*, narrow, and Latin *angere*, to strangle.

**Ask** P.J. McCall, the author of the ballad *Boolavogue*, which commemorates the Rising of 1798, heard *ask* for a newt in Co. Carlow. From Old English *athexe* a lizard, this.

**Ax** People write to me frequently asking about what they consider to be the ignorant way in which the word *ax*, as used in phrases such as **he axed me out**, have survived all the attempts of schooling to eradicate it. Well, although *ax* is now, unfortunately, considered a vulgarism everywhere, thank goodness for the word's survival, because it has as long a pedigree as *ask*, and is still in constant use all over the English-speaking world.

'I am often axed to tell it, sir,' says a character in Crofton Croker's *Fairy Legends and Traditions of the South of Ireland*, back in 1862. Twenty years later, Tennyson, in one of his sometimes comical forays into the field of dialect poetry, wrote this as an example of Lincolnshire speech: 'Summun 'ed hax'd fur a son, an 'e promised a son to shee.' 'Axe and it shall be geven you,' was Tindale's 1526 translation of *Matthew* VII, 7. 'How sholde I axen mercy of Tisbe?' axed Chaucer in *The Legend of Good Women*. Wyclif in 1388 wrote 'Whanne he schal axe, what shal Y answere to hym?' in his translation of *Job*. A long and distinguished pedigree, indeed. *Ax* comes from Old English *acsian*, to ask. Down to about 1600 *ax*, found mostly in southern England, was the common literary form; thereafter the northern *ask*, from Old English *ascian*, began to replace it. The Teutonic words have a pedigree dating back to Sanskrit, which has *ish*, to seek, and *ichchhá*, wish.

**Baffity** A Carlow woman of my acquaintance was having coffee in Kilkenny city one day when she overheard a conversation between two women of a certain age, as they say. They were giving out about the younger generation, and one of them remarked that 'young ones don't mind being seen in any class of oul' baffity nowadays.' *Baffity* is a

word I myself have never heard outside of
Kilkenny. It is a cheap, generally cotton fabric,
originally of oriental manufacture. Seamus Moylan
in *The Language of Kilkenny* has 'She'd take a lot of
baffity for a shift', used of a large lady. As to origin,
it is from the Persian *baft*, wove.

**Baigle** A friend of mine, a Cork city man,
overheard two men discussing the life and hard
times of an acquaintance in a west Cork public
house, and one mentioned the baigle of the woman
he was married to. Baigle is a variant of *beagle*, and
the *English Dialect Dictionary* has this to say about
it: 'An opprobrious epithet applied to a depraved,
unmanagable, and troublesome person'. It is found
in the northern counties of England and in
Shakespeare's Warwickshire. As is the case in west
Cork, it is applied to women, and to difficult
children, by men.

A beagle is a hunting dog, as the world knows.
The word is not from the modern French, as is
commonly thought; their *bigle* is borrowed from
English, in fact. It is not from Old English either,
because of the hard *g*. So where did the word
originate? The Oxford Dictionary does not rule out
the theory that the word is from the Old French
*beeguelle*, a noisy, shouting person, a word derived
from *beer*, to gape, open wide, plus *guele*, throat.
That makes sense.

**Barge** A dialect verb which means to abuse verbally, *to barge*, is found all over Ireland. It is common in Scotland and England as well. 'An' the girl kep bargein' an' bangin' him with the beesom' (*brush*), wrote the author of *A Fenian's Night Entertainment* of a hard-pressed Leinsterman in the late nineteenth century. Seán O'Casey has 'She was bargin out of her' in *The Plough and the Stars*. J.M. Synge has the word in *The Shanachie*. It has been suggested that here we have a back formation from *barge*, the river craft, as bargees were noted for using rather crude language. Perhaps. The word doesn't appear in literature before the nineteenth century, at any rate.

**Bevy** I have heard over the years many interesting words and phrases in the north of Co. Dublin, in the district known as Fingall (*Fine Gall*, territory of the foreigners, who happened to be Scandinavians). A lady once wrote to tell me that the young men used to call the women who stood apart from the men in the ballrooms of romance of the 1950s *a bevy*. This collective noun was applied to women as far back as the fifteenth century, and in the sixteenth Spenser referred to 'this bevie of ladies bright' in *The Shephearde's Calendar*. *Bevy* today can mean a flock of quail or a herd of roebuck; Spenser used the word figuratively and we are indebted to Thomas Nashe, his near contemporary, for the explanation that 'the terme is taken of larkes.' A lovely, complimentary term if ever I heard one.

**Breeze** An interesting word I heard from a Traveller in Co. Kildare was this *breeze*. I thought the word might be from their cant, or secret language, called variously Sheldru, Shelta, Gammon, and Minker's Tawrie, but it isn't. *Breeze*, a horsefly, although not found in the speech of settled people, is a dialect word known from Northumberland to Gloucestershire, and here in Ireland only to horse-copers. Mr Connors, a Traveller of Wexford descent, was relating with an amount of glee understandable in the circumstances, how he was frustrated in selling a mare to a nervous lady rider who had backed the animal. 'A breeze bit the mare in the arse,' explained my friend, 'and med her take off like the divil from hell was after her.'

This is an old word. Chaucer has it as *breese* in *Balade*, written c. 1380: 'I wol me venge on loue as doth a breese/ On sylde horsse,' a sentiment Mr Connors would understand. Shakespeare, in *Troilus and Cressida* has: 'The herd hath more annoyance by the breese than by the tiger.' The word is in Old English as *briosa* and *breosa*.

Another interesting *breeze*. An old man from Carne in Co. Wexford, Phil Wall, who was in his nineties when I met him in 1970, called perspiration *breeze*. A midlands Englishman might recognise breeze as the moisture which fogs up his car windscreen. 'Of unknown origin', say the few dictionaries to have recorded the word.

**Cave** To my mind, one of the nastiest faults you'll find in a child's pony is a propensity to **cave**, that is, to stretch his neck towards the ground and to bring it back up again suddenly; an action that can break a nose or knock a child unconscious. I smiled when I saw the greatest flat jockey of them all deal with a caving horse down at the stalls at the Curragh; he gave the animal a smart whack of his stick between the ears and the caper suddenly ended. Not a practice I approve of, of course, but it worked. The verb *cave* is known to Travellers who deal in horses; I've heard it from settled Ulster and Connacht horse-copers as well. In Co. Louth it is used of cattle who push other cattle before them with their heads; and in England the verb has been defined as 'to paw the ground, rear, plunge, as a horse'.

These additional shades of meaning make sense etymologically, even if they are unknown to the horse-copers I am privileged to know; the verb is, in all probability, from the Old Norse *kaf*, a plunge.

**Chavel** Not far from where I live in Co. Wicklow I heard a farmer use this verb. He was speaking of the damage rats did to his store of oats; they had chavelled in under the floorboards, and then they had chavelled the oats. The dialect dictionaries tell me that the word, which means to gnaw, nibble, tear with the teeth, is confined to Yorkshire, Derbyshire, Lincolnshire, and Leicestershire, and even the great *English Dialect Dictionary* failed to record it from Ireland. That is surprising, as it is to be found in Wexford, Carlow, Kildare and Wicklow. I've often heard horsemen from these counties speak of a horse chavelling the bit. There is a noun **chavellings**, the fragments of what has been gnawed or nibbled, and the verbal noun, chavelling, chattering, 'jawing', is found in *The Owl and the Nightingale*, which dates from before 1250. I was glad to find that D.H. Lawrence had no scruples about using this old dialect word in *The White Peacock*: 'The bracken lay sere under the trees, broken and chavelled by the restless wild winds of the long winter.' *Chavel* is from Middle English *chauel*, the jaw, jowl, cheek; itself from the Old English *ceafl*.

**Childer** Many people in rural Ireland, north, south, east and west, refer to children as **childer**. The old word, I'm glad to say, is unlikely to die out. It has also survived in general dialect use in England, and in Scotland where *bairns* is not used. Tennyson, in a misguided attempt to do for Ireland what William Barnes did for Dorset, wrote, in a tear-jerker called *To-Morrow*, 'Him and his childer wor keenin' as if he had lost them all.'

There is a book to be written on the comparative folklore of words. Holy Innocents'

Day, 28 December, was known in Co. Wexford as **Childermas Day**, and was regarded as the unluckiest day of the year. So unlucky, in fact, that the day of the year on which it falls was marked as a black day for the whole year to come. This notion is not confined to the south-east of Co. Wexford, the Baronies of Forth and Bargy, where no important affair was taken in hand on Childermas Day, and where going on a sea voyage or entering a house never previously entered was considered madness. To this day many Cornish housewives refrain from washing anything on this day, and I am reliably informed that news of a wedding in the Cornish town of Newquay was greeted by some old-timers last year with gasps of astonishment. This fear of the day which marks Herod's slaughter of the Innocents was mentioned as far back as 1711 in London's *Spectator*: 'No, child, you shall not begin upon Childermas Day; tell your master that Friday will be soon enough.' Anyway *childer* is Middle English. Wyclif has 'praise ye childer, the Lord' in his translation of the *Psalms* (1382).

**Chitter** 'They come in here every Friday to chitter', complained an old malt-worm in a Dungarvan, Co. Waterford, hostelry to me recently. He was complaining about four women who disturb his peace on their way home from playing golf.

*Chitter* is a parallel form of 'chatter', used commonly of bird-song. Joyce used it of running water in *Finnegans Wake*: 'Can't hear with the waters of, the chittering waters of.' The word is common along the east coast, too. It is also found in Scotland, the north of England, and in Devon and Cornwall. Chaucer in *The Miller's Tale* has: 'Of hir song, it was so lowd and yerne/ As eny swelwe chittering on a berse.'

*Chitter* has another meaning. In rural Fermanagh to chitter means to shiver with the cold. I've heard this meaning in Donegal, too, at the back of Errigal mountain. John Skelton knew it in 1526: 'Se for God avowe, for cold as I chydder'; and Robert Burns, over two hundred years later, has 'The birds sit chittering in the thorn', in *Cauld Blaws the Wind*.

**Cod; all a cod** You won't have to look far in Ireland to find the word *cod* used, in phrases such as **that's all a cod**. *Cod*, noun, is a hoax, humbug, an imposition, a lie; hence the equally common **cod-acting**, tomfoolery. This *cod* is the same word as the Old English *cod*, a bag. The old advertisers could be just as brash as their modern counterparts who advertise items of female hygiene on television: a tract called *Brunswyke's Distylled Waters*, written in 1527, assured its readers that the product was 'good for mannes yards or coddes'. In what way? you might ask. I don't know, but I can guess. So it seems that the Kerry word for a football, **caid**, is Teutonic in origin.

**Collogue** is still common in Ireland. It means to conspire; to talk confidentially, usually for the purpose of making mischief. As a noun it simply means a confidential chat. Oxford says that it is almost obsolete in English. Milton has the first meaning given above in *Ikonoklastes*, written in 1649: 'He never durst from that time doe otherwise than ... collogue with the Pope and his adherants.' Earlier, in 1602, the dramatist Beaumont has the second meaning, a chat, in *Salmacis*: 'To him she went, and so collogues that night/ With the best straines of pleasure's sweet delight.'

The word, common in the works of Carleton, Emily Lawless, Jane Barlow, and in more recent times, Peadar O'Donnell, is, in all probability, from the French noun *colloque*, a conference.

**Crick** You'll hear the word *crick* for a spasm in either the neck or back in most Irish dialects. It is in general dialect use in England too, and I find it strange indeed that, considering how commonly used it is, it has been relegated to dialect status in some dictionaries. *Crick* is old and is of uncertain origin. It is probably onomatopoeic, imitative of the sudden jerk the spasm causes, the Oxford Dictionary says. One of the oldest of the language's dictionaries, the 1440 *Promptorium Parvulorum*

*Sive Clericorum*, defined *crykke* as 'spasmus', and John Florio's Italian-English dictionary, *A Worlde of Wordes*, the second edition of which was dedicated to James the First's queen, Anne of Denmark, has: 'Adolomato: troubled with a cricke or wrinche in the necke or backe'. That the word is from the Irish *creach*, plunder, is nonsense.

**Croodle** is a lovely word. It means to cuddle. In deepest Carlow, in the beautiful village of St Mullins by the banks of the Barrow, I once heard an old man tease a young fellow who was off courting: 'I suppose you are goin' up now to croodle with the young wan.' The word is Teutonic in origin. Compare the Middle English *crodle*, pronounced with a long *o*; the Middle Dutch *crúdan*, and the Old English verb *crúden*, to press, crowd. The word may also be heard in Ulster.

**Crud** This is a word sent to me by a Monaghan woman. She makes cheese. Her mother called cottage cheese **crud cheese**. *Crudde* is a Middle English form of *curd*. *Crud* is common in northern England and in Scotland.

**Delf**, often spelled **delph**, is a word used extensively in Ireland for earthenware and crockery. I have seen it written that the word is confined to Hiberno-English but this is not so; it is common still in England's North Country and in parts of Scotland. Its origin is the Dutch town of *Delf* (the

*t* was added to the town's name in Middle Dutch
for no good reason) which was named from the
*delf*, ditch, by which the chief canal of the town is
still known. Middle English has *delf* for ditch, from
Late Old English *dælf*, trench, ditch, quarry,
apparently from *gedelf*, a digging, a ditch, from
*delfan*, to delve or dig. As far as is known, Swift
was the first Irishman to use *delf* in print. In his
*Poems to Stella at Woodpark*, written in 1723, he
has, 'A supper worthy of herself,/ Five nothings in
five plates of delf.'

**Dinge** Some time ago a man from Kent who
lives near me asked me about the word **dinge**. He
had been shopping, and an honest Wicklowman
came to tell him that he had put a dinge in his car's
boot by backing into it in the car park. *Dinge*
noun, an indentation, a dent, and *dinge* verb, to
indent, knock in, I was astounded to hear, are not
in the vocabulary of southern England. I went
home to my dialect dictionaries. They confirmed
that the word is found only in Ireland, Scotland,
and the northern counties of England, and that it
is unknown south of Cheshire and Lincolnshire.

*Dinge* first appeared in literature in Randle
Cotgrave's French-English dictionary of 1611. It
has: 'Bosseler, to dindge, to bruise, to make a dint
in vessel of metall, or in a peece of plate'. Our
word possibly represents an earlier, unattested
*denge*, from Old Norse *dengja*, to hammer, beat.

The ever-cautious Oxford Dictionary tentatively suggests that a later onomatopoeic origin from *dint* seems possible. *Dint* and its phonetic variant *dent* are from Old English *dynt*, cognate with Old Norse *dyntr*, a stroke or blow, especially one given in swordplay.

**Donnybrook** is a father and mother of an organised fight between factions. It has also been defined as a wild, drunken revel in which a large crowd participates. I've heard the word in America and in Britain. It is named from a suburb of Dublin, a very respectable one nowadays, I might add. In the nineteenth century Donnybrook was a village cut off from the capital, and it was the centre of a great fair which was noted for its fights with shillelaghs, and a major tourist attraction.

The celebrated German Prince von Puckler-Muskau visited the fair in 1828. He saw a few drunken fights, but nothing serious; he left early. 'The poverty, the dirt, and the wild tumult were as great as the glee and merriment with which the cheapest pleasures were enjoyed,' he wrote. 'There were many hundred tents, all ragged like the people, and adorned with tawdry rags instead of flags; one had hoisted a dead and half-putrid cat as a sign. The lowest sort of rope-dancers and posture-masters exercised their toilsome vocation on stages of planks, and dressed in shabby finery, dancing and grimacing in the dreadful heat until they were completely exhausted. A third part of the public lay, or rather rolled about, drunk; others ate, screamed, shouted and fought … As I left the fair, a pair of lovers, excessively drunk, took the same road. It was a rich treat to watch their behaviour. Both were horribly ugly, but treated each other with the greatest tenderness, and the most delicate attention. The lover especially displayed a sort of chivalrous politeness. Nothing could be more gallant, and at the same time more respectful, as his repeated efforts to prevent his fair one from falling, although he had no little difficulty in keeping his own balance … Don't reproach me for the vulgarity of the pictures I send you: they are more akin to nature than the painted dolls of our salons.'

**Elder** More than once correspondents have asked me about this farmers' word, which is common all over Ireland in place of the *udder* of a cow or mare. Patrick Kennedy from Wexford, in his *Fireside Stories* of 1870, has: 'A cow with her poor elder so full that it was trailing on the ground'. The word is found all over Scotland and in England from the border counties as far south as Leicestershire and the West Country. It is from Middle Dutch *elder*, 'a teate, a mamme or dugge', according to Henry Hexham's *Copious English and Netherduytch Dictionary* of 1647, recently republished in facsimile.

*Udder*, by the way, is not a related word. It is found in old English in a tract dated 1000, as *úder*; the Old Norse form is *júgr*; the Middle Dutch *uyder*.

**Element** 'I took them for some faery vision,/ Of some gay creatures of the element,' wrote John Milton in *Comus*. The lines reminded me that I've heard *element* meaning the sky, atmosphere, heavens, firmament, in the fishing village of Kilmore, Co. Wexford. Not *elements*, mind you, but used in the singular, as Milton used it. The first time I heard it was back in 1970, from an old fisherman with the illustrious name William Blake. Another fisherman, Jack Devereux, a man who was a major informant on matters of dialect, also used element as Milton did, and as Thomas Hardy probably used it: 'The element looks nice and blue this morning' was recorded in Dorset. Yorkshire people also use this element when they speak of the sky: Michael Parkinson would well understand somebody who might remark, 'The element looks fearful heavisome.'

*Element* is used figuratively in Ireland, but as far as I can tell, this is not the case across the water. *The Folklore Journal* of 1886 recorded 'that's the element!' in Donegal. It adds a gloss: 'Intended to indicate that what is going on is above the common; especially when describing music'. The *English Dialect Dictionary* recorded 'He has a great element for shooting', in Westmeath, and Patrick Kennedy in *The Banks of the Boro* (1867) has this from Wexford: 'If he happens to have reached the quarrelsome stage of his element …' We've all heard somebody or other who was 'in his, or her, element' – in the same stage of command as Kennedy's man. *Element* is from Old French *element*, from Latin *elementum*, of which the etymology and the primary meaning are uncertain, but which was employed as a translation of a Greek word which had various meanings, including a member of the planetary system. The sense of Milton's *element*, and Bill Blake's, is due to the medieval Latin *elementum ignis* as the name of a fiery, starry sphere, a comet.

**Elf** This is a type of fairy, and the word, as far as I know, is not commonly found in Hiberno-English except in the compounds **elf-shot** and **elf-stones**. *Elf-shot* is found in the north and in Westmeath, Meath and Louth. Carleton tells us that 'if a man had a sick cow, she was elf-shot.' What he meant was that she had been struck with little flint arrows, called *elf-shot*, by the fairies. Scott, in his *Minstrelsy*, says that the approved cure is to chafe the parts affected with a blue bonnet. In Munster, the flint arrows used by the fairies to cause disease were called *elf-stones*, Crofton Croker tells us in his *Fairy Legends*. In Wexford in the old days an **elf-bolt** was said to be the cause of disease in both cattle and humans. Brontë has this word in

*Wuthering Heights.* Small world. The Anglo-Saxon *Leechdoms* of c. 1000 has *ylfa gescot* as the name of a disease caused by the little pests, so the belief is ancient, and seems to be Teutonic in origin.

**Faction fights**, at which the *shillelagh* (q.v.) was used to murderous effect, took place at **patterns,** fairs held on local saints' feast days. *Pattern* is from English *patron*, from the Norman French *patron*, by the way; the Catholic hierarchy banned many of them in the early nineteenth century because, as the Bishop of Cork said when he shut down the medieval pattern at Gougane Barra in the west Cork mountains in 1818, 'the pattern was selected for the purpose of contest by hostile factions.' Sometimes these factions were outlawed agrarian groups anxious to show their mettle; others were family fighting family just for the fun of it; sometimes town factions came to country patterns to issue their challenges.

Henry Inglis came to Ireland from Scotland in 1834 and saw a faction fight in Connemara. He left a whiskey tent after a challenge had been delivered and accepted, and sat on a rock at a safe distance: 'I had not long to wait,' he wrote. 'Out sallied the Joyces and a score of other "boys" from several tents at once, as if there had been some preconcerted signal; and the flourishing of shillelaghs did not long precede the using of them. Any one to see an Irish fight for the first time would conclude that a score or two must inevitably be put *hors de combat*. The very flourish of a regular shillelagh, and the shout that accompanies it, seem to be the immediate precursors of a fractured skull; but the affair, though bad enough, is not so fatal as it appears to be: the shillelaghs, no doubt, sometimes do descend upon a head, which is forthwith a broken head; but they oftener descend upon each other and the fight soon becomes one of personal strength. The parties close and graple; and the most powerful man throws his adversary; fair play is but little attended to; two or three often attack a single man; nor is there a cessation of blows even when a man is on the ground. On the present occasion five or six were disabled, but there was no homicide … I noticed, after the fight, that some, who had been opposed to each other, shook hands and kissed; and appeared to be as good friends as before.'

**Fadaise** Within the space of a week I once got two letters about this interesting word. One was from Co. Clare, near the border with Galway. It was, until recently, an Irish-speaking district and the word sent to me from there for identification was spelled by its sender *faidéis*. It means, I was told, nonsensical talk, twaddle. I was sure it was an Irish word; but not a trace could I find of it in any dictionary. The native speakers of the language I consulted were as mystified as I was.

Then came letter number two, this time from Swords in north Co. Dublin. A lady there wanted to know something about a word she spelled *fwadaysh*, a pronunciation identical with *faidéis*. And, I was informed, the word also meant nonsensical talk, a stupid remark. This time, the letter gave me the clue I needed. Its sender said that it was one of her grandfather's words; he was an old soldier from the Great War era who had a lot of barrack-room slang. This was no slang word, I recognised belatedly, but the French *fadaise*, meaning 'twaddle, nonsense'.

**Fascination** Some of the older people, versed in the ways of the countryside, will tell you how stoats *fascinate* small birds and animals, sometimes simply by staring at them, denying them the power of movement, until the vicious predator can come close enough to strike. Many's the time I've heard Wexford and south Kilkenny people use *fascinate* in this sense. Snakes, I am told, are past masters at it.

*Fascination* is connected with witchcraft; now, thank God, the ancient connection has been forgotten, and the word is used only in social compliment these days. But in the seventeenth century a man couldn't tell a woman she fascinated him without sending shivers down her spine. *Fascination* has undergone a change of meaning since it was borrowed from the Latin *fascinare*, to enchant, itself from the noun *fascinum*, spell, witchcraft. To be accused of fascination in Tudor or Jacobean times could easily have led to the stake. Burton in his *Anatomy of Melancholy* written between 1621 and 1651, asks: 'Why do witches and old women fascinate and bewitch children?' The fascination was supposedly done by casting the evil eye on them.

**Firkle** This word is a term of contempt I've heard in Kildare and in Limerick where the Palatines came to seek refuge from religious persecution in the eighteenth century. It means a dirty person. It has also reached Down and Antrim, and can be found in the old glossaries compiled in these two counties. As you may have guessed from the southern Palatine connection, the word is of German origin. It came into English from the Low German *ferkle*, a little pig, which gave the identical word in modern German.

**Fleam** God rest John Doyle, the miller of Old Ross, Co. Wexford, who died recently in his nineties. Not long before he died he sent me some old milling words. One was *fleam*, a mill race. I had heard this in my youth in St Mullins, in Co. Carlow, where there was a milling tradition dating back 1,300 years, to the time of St Moling, who is reputed to have comforted the dying Suibhne, the hard-pressed king of Dal nAraide, near his own fleam by the Barrow. Seamus Heaney has given us

a beautiful translation of the medieval legend,
*Sweeney Astray*, as no doubt you know.

At any rate, fleam is from Middle English *flum*,
from Latin *flumen*, a river. This appears to be the
oldest meaning of the word. A manuscript from
1300, *St Margarete*, refers to 'the fleme iurdan'
(*Jordan*). Later, perhaps about 1500, the word
came to be used specifically of a mill race.
Fitzherbert's *Survey* of 1523 speaks of a 'mylne
fleme made with mens hande'.

**Flick** Another great survival found in the
English of Co. Waterford is *flick*. You and I would
call it a *flitch*. *Flick* has its origin in Old English
*flicce*, a side of bacon, salted and cured,
corresponding to the Old Norse *flikki*. A glossary
from c. 700 has 'Perna, flicci'. *Perna* is the Latin
for a gammon. John Skelton in *Colin Cloute*
(c. 1529) refers to a 'bacon flycke'; and nearer our
own time George Eliot in her *Adam Bede* has
'Thou lookst as white as a bacon flick.'

**Fog-full** is an expression you'll hear in Carlow,
said of a person who has eaten too much. This *fog*
seems to be related to the adjective *foggy*, glossed by
Palsgrave back in 1530 as 'to (*too*) ful of waste
flesshe'. John Skelton in *Elynour Rummyng* (1529)
has: 'All foggy fat she was.' I was not surprised at
hearing of this *fog* compound in Carlow, as Patrick
Kennedy from my own Wexford has one like it in

*The Banks of the Boro*, written in 1867: 'Somehow or other we did not sleep easy after this **fog-meal**.' How they came to the south-east is anybody's guess; the dictionaries record them only in northern Scotland and in Ulster, where W.H. Patterson in his Antrim and Down glossary of 1880 has: 'A person who has eaten too much is said to have got a **fog-fill**. Carleton, like Patrick Kennedy, has *fog-meal*: 'The bride herself made nothing less than a right fog-meal of it.' Seamus Heaney tells me that *fog* means moss in south Derry.

Apparently *fog* is connected with the dialect word *fog* meaning aftermath, the grass which springs up immediately after the hay has been taken off a field. Rich and nutritious, it may bloat animals who eat it; hence the adjective **foggy** fat, puffy. The word is of unknown origin. The Welsh *ffwg* dry grass is often given (especially by the Welsh), but I can put a dinge in that theory: *ffwg* is from English.

**Fricker** In Graiguenamanagh, that beautiful village on the banks of the Barrow in Co. Kilkenny, I met a man from the Connors clan of Travelling horse-dealers who described a pony he was leading 'as a real little fricker'. Just to be sure that I heard the word properly I asked Mr Connors to repeat the word. 'A fricker, boss,' he said, 'a lively little divil.' I looked at the dialect dictionaries when I got home. Not a trace could I find in the

Irish glossaries, but this little treasure of a word is found all over southern England, and it has a pedigree longer than Secretariat's or Galileo's, not to mention my friend's pony's. It is from the Old English *frician*, to move briskly, to dance. An extraordinary dialect survival.

**Frim** A young woman from a Travelling clan came to my door looking for scrap, and assured me that I was looking **frim**. She kindly glossed the word for me, seeing my puzzled expression. 'Frim, in good fettle, thriving', she said, and then added, 'handsome', the minx. I had never heard the word, and it seems to be confined to Travellers; but it is common in the dialects of England, where they also have the word in the following senses: of crops, luxuriant in growth, early, forward; of animals, in heat, or *brimming*, as they say where Shakespeare grew up; of bees, about to swarm. The word is from the Old English *freme*, cognate with *fram*, forward, advanced, bold. It is in *Beowulf*, I see.

**Frump** is a word I've heard used in Co. Kildare. In that part of the world, famed for its stud farms and racehorses, a *frump* is a bad-tempered old woman. I've also found this meaning in Wexford and Waterford, and it is common in Scotland, in northern and midland England, as well as in Somerset and Hampshire. Dickens has this frump in *Our Mutual Friend*: 'Don't fancy me a frumpy old married woman.' Of course he might have had another meaning in mind: the common Irish meaning of slovenly in dress and habits, but I don't think so. At any rate the origin of both these frumps is probably the verb *frumple*, to wrinkle, itself from the Dutch *verrompelen*, of the same meaning. Frumple's first appearance in literature is in the 1398 translation by John de Trevisa of a Latin medical tract. John tells his readers that 'the flesshe in the buttocks is fromplyd and knotty.' Now you know.

The only other *frump* that has come to my notice is the one found in the Baronies of Forth and Bargy in south-east Wexford. It is a verb which means to jeer, to make fun of. It is common in Scotland, and in the northern and midland dialects of England; and it is common, too, in the southern dialects of Dorset, Pembrokeshire, Devon and Cornwall, from which it may have reached Wexford, through the age-old contacts of fishing fleets. Possibly connected with *frumple*, some say. Beaumont and Fletcher have this *frump* as a noun in *The Scornful Lady*, first performed in the year of Shakespeare's death, 1616: 'Sweet widow, leave your frumps and be edified.' It is clear from the context of the sentence that the lady was a scoffer.

**Frush, Fell** I was reminded recently of these good words used by people who keep horses. A few of us were discussing a big English race meeting, and one wise man in the company shook his head when I told him that I was going to invest a small sum on a certain animal bred by a friend of mine. He had heard, he said, that the horse in question was off recently, the result of a tender *frush*, also commonly called the frog.

The word *frush* is common in the dialects of northern England and its etymology has been bothering lexicographers for a long time. Some dictionaries say that the word is related to the Scots and Northumberland adjective *frush* which means brittle. But this cannot be so; that word was not recorded before the nineteenth century.

An old writer on equine matters, Edward Topsell, who flourished in Shakespeare's time, may have the answer for us. In *The Historie of Four-Footed Beastes* he wrote: 'The frush is the tenderest part of the hoof towards the heel, and because it is fashioned like a forked head the French men call it Furchetto, to which our farriers, perhaps for easiness sake of pronunciation, do make it a monosyllable and pronounce it frush.'

*Fell* is a noun I have heard from Wexford Travellers who deal with horses. 'He's worth the price of his fell and no more,' I heard one of them say at Ballinasloe, Co. Galway, horse fair. *Fell* is skin. It is common to this day in Scotland and in the northern and midland dialects of England. It is from Middle English *felle*, from Old English *fel*, a skin.

**Fubsy** I heard this old word **fubsy** in Greystones, Co. Wicklow, recently. This is obviously an import from England, but the woman I heard it from was a Wicklow woman of the old stock. It means stout, portly. **Fobby** is a variant. Sir Thomas More has this; gluttony, he said, 'maketh the body fat and fobby'. My Greystones friend told me that *fubsy* is not used to describe a woman; neither is it a term of derision. Ivor Brown, the Scots lexicographer, wrote that *fubsy* should not be used of men of Falstaffian appearance. The man who larded the lean earth as he walked along outranged the term altogether. *Fubsy* is for small, plump men, but not for adiposity's masterpiece.

**Gick, geck, gink** The contemptuous term **gick** came my way from Waterford. It means a stupid, clumsy fellow. You'll hear its variant **geck** in your travels, especially in Carlow, Wexford and south Tipperary. It was imported from England, where it is common in Staffordshire, Leicestershire, Yorkshire and Cornwall. Shakespeare had it in *Twelfth Night*: 'The most notorious geck and gull/ That e'er invention played on.' George Eliot, too, has it in *Adam Bede*: 'If she's tackled to a geck as everybody's a-laughin' at …' The origin of the word is the Dutch *geck*, 'a foole', according to Henry Hexham's English-Dutch dictionary of 1647.

*Gick* and *geck* should not be confused with *gink*, a term of reproach applied only to a girl considered flighty by oldies in the south-eastern counties. I cannot find the word in the dialect dictionaries, though there is a Scottish *ginkie*, a term of reproach applied to a lighthearted girl. And then there's the American slang *gink*, a pejorative term used only in reference to men: this, too, has reached Ireland and England. P.G. Wodehouse has it in *A Damsel in Distress*: 'I'm certain this gink is giving her a raw deal.' Perhaps this *gink*, too, is from the Scots *ginkie*.

**Git** This is a very common expression of contempt. It means, of course, offspring, progeny, especially a person born out of wedlock; an unruly brat; an eejit. It is a variant of *get*, and this is from the Old Norse *geta*, to beget.

The old Scots poets were also very fond of *git* as a term of opprobrium. They used to pull no punches in having a go in print at other practitioners, and Cranstoun's edition of the *Satirical Poems* (1567) contains the marvellous first line: 'Blasphemus baird and beggiris gitt'.

**Gite** A lady whose mother comes from Tramore in Co. Waterford sent me an ancient word which I have myself known since childhood. 'Will you look at the gite of her,' said the old lady, on seeing a picture of a near-naked fashion model. *Gite* is an extraordinary survival, still used in the south west of England in the sense 'dress'. Chaucer has 'She cam after in a gyte of reed' in *The Reeve's Tale*. John

Skelton in *Elynour Rummyng*, written about 1529, has 'When she doth her aray/ And gyrdeth in her gytes:/ Stytched and praked wyth pletes.' The Old French has *guite*, an article of clothing; a hat.

**Gudget** In Carlow, Kilkenny, west Wexford and west Waterford a glutton is called a *gudget* by country people. A farmer friend who lives not far from Dungarvan, Co. Waterford once complained to me that a gudget he had working for him would eat a horse for his breakfast. Seamus Moylan has the word in *The English of Kilkenny*; he quotes an informant who explained the word as 'a little selfish lump of a person, especially in respect of food'.

Across the water gudget is found in Scotland and in northern England. It is related to the verb *gudge*, to stuff, to eat ravenously, but the original meaning seems to be a camp follower, hence a menial or low type. The word's origin is the French *gouget*. Andrew Duncan's *Appendix Etymologiae* of 1595 defines the word as a burden-bearer.

**Haaf-boat** An English visitor to a Cork fishing port which in summer looks like Cowes or Cannes, wrote to me about a term he heard there from an old fisherman who was describing a craft that could, he had little doubt, get him safely around Cape Horn. This wasn't a little half-decker, mind you, nor indeed a modern trawler, but a splendidly equipped racing yacht. My correspondent wrote the word as *half-boat*, but what he heard, I'm sure, was **haaf-boat**, a term used in Shetland and in Scotland, as well as in some of the Irish fishing ports.

I heard the term myself in Kilmore Quay from old Bill Blake, a seaman of note, and an authority on the old Wexford ketches, now no longer built. I remember writing it down myself in error as *half-boat*. A *haaf-boat* is one suitable for sailing far out in the deep-sea. *Haaf* means the open sea, the deep-sea fishing ground. The word is from the Old Norse *haf*, the sea. It survives in modern Swedish as *haf*, and in Norwegian and Danish as *hav*.

**Hefty** One of the most frightening seas I have ever seen was running between Carnsore Point and Kilmore Quay, Co. Wexford, when I went for a walk along the beach there in the depths of last winter. This coast was known in the old days as the graveyard of a thousand ships and I could see why. When I called into a local hostelry, The Lobster Pot, for something warm afterwards, an old man said, 'Hefty weather, ain't it?' It had been a long time since I had heard this adjective *hefty*, not the hefty which means heavy, a late derivative of *heave*, but an obsolete form from the Dutch *heftigh*, violent. The related German is *heftig*.

**Hind** I once witnessed an incident in a Carlow hotel restaurant, involving a waitress who used a word bordering on the obsolete, I should think, to describe a customer. The gentleman in question, previous to a dignified and unhurried departure, had told her that a local politician, who was at the time drowning his sorrows with some election workers at the bar, had kindly insisted on paying for his substantial dinner, well washed down with some expensive-looking claret. It became obvious some time after he left that this was not the case. She called the duplicitous one, who was not known to her, **a right hind**; what your man, the unsuccessful county council candidate, called him when presented with the bill, you may guess.

A *hind* is a boyo, a rascal. I had heard the word in my youth in west Wexford and in south Carlow, by the banks of the lordly river Barrow. The word is common still in Scotland and England, but I note that the Irish shade of meaning has been recorded only in Norfolk. In both Scotland and the northern counties of England a *hind* was, in the old days, a farm labourer engaged by the year, and provided with a house, firing, milk, meal and potatoes. Little or no money changed hands. Often a stipulation was made that the hind must furnish a female farm labourer as well, usually a wife or daughter, at an agreed price per day, with an extra wage at harvest time. She was called a *bondager*.

From *hind* came the adjective *hindish*, rustic, clumsy, clownish, and of course, my waitress's word. The word's prevalence in the speech and literature of Scotland would suggest that it must also be found in Ulster, but I've never come across it there, and neither can I find any mention of it in the province's dialect dictionaries. *Hind* was formed from the Old English *hi(g)na*, genitive plural of *hiwa*, *higa*, member of a family; a servant. The *d* is excrescent.

**Hooligan, hooley** I am often asked about the origin of these words. Many people think the two words are related. The origin of both words is unascertained, according to Oxford. *Hooley* first appeared in print in Bartlett's *Dictionary of American English* in 1877, spelled *huly*, and described as a noise, an uproar. It also gave the phrase *to raise huly*. Many's the time I've read that this *huly/hooley* gave rise to *hooligan*, but this is based on folk-etymology, which says that London police courts reports of 1898 refer to *Hooley's Gang*; unfortunately, no positive confirmation of this has been discovered by researchers. In a *Daily News* item printed on 8 August 1898, we find 'The constable said the prisoner belonged to a gang of rough youths calling themselves Hooligans.' But this comparatively harmless gang may have taken its name either from a music hall song of 1880 which described the doings of a rowdy Irish family, the Hooligans, or from a character of the same name who appeared in a series of adventures in *Funny Folks*, a popular journal of the day. An earlier citation gives a farce by T.G. Rodwell, first performed in 1824, and called

*More Blunders Than One*, which featured a drunken Irish butler named Larry O'Hoolagan. Better to side with Oxford and say that both *hooley* and *hooligan* are of uncertain lineage.

**Ill** As I was sitting in the lounge of a Wexford hotel watching a game of hurling on the television recently, the man at my side, commenting on the antics of a certain player, said that he was **ill**. I could discern no indisposition, except perhaps a mental one which caused him to strike out wildly at ever opponent in sight; an inquiry led to the explanation that *ill* meant not sick, but headstrong. I thought since of Shakespeare's various *ills*. *Bad*: 'I told thee they were ill for a green wound', in *Henry IV*, part 2. *Inauspicious*: 'There's some ill planet reigns', in *A Winter's Tale*. *Adverse*: 'Against ill chances men are ever merry', *Henry IV*, part 2. *Sick*: 'He that made me knows I see thee ill', in *Richard the Second*. *Incompetent*: I am ill at these numbers', in *Hamlet*.

All these meanings may still be heard in various Irish dialects. The Wexford shade of meaning has been in English since the eleventh century. Its origin, and the origin of all the other *ills* is the Old Norse *illr*, bad.

**Jackeen** Brendan Behan wouldn't have taken offence if you called him this. The Jackeen is your real Dubliner, bred, born and reared; he is a working man. The term was first used back in the nineteenth century when Mr and Mrs Samuel Carter Hall, those perceptive observers of Ireland immediately before the Famine, told us about him as he was then, a useless layabout: 'The number of idlers in the busy world is fearfully large; from the *walking gentleman* of the upper ranks, to the *half-sir* of the middle, and the *Jackeen* of the class a little above the lower; the *walking gentleman* being always elegantly attired, of course always unemployed, with ample leisure for the studies which originate depravity; the *half-sir* being, generally, a younger brother, with little or no income of his own, and so educated as to be deprived, utterly, of the energy and self-dependence which create usefulness, the "Masther Tom", who broke the dogs, shot the crows, first backed the vicious horse …; the *Jackeen* being a production found everywhere, but most abundantly in large towns … The Jackeen might have been seen – regularly a few years ago, and now occasionally – at eary morning lounging against the (Trinity) college rails, with the half-intoxicated, half-insolent air that betokens a night passed in debauch; his stockings, that had once been white, falling from under the drab-green, ill-fitting trousers over the shoes; his coat usually of green; his waistcoat of some worn and faded finery; and the segment of collar that peeped over the stock, fashionable in cut, but not in quality, was crushed and degraded from its original property; his hat, always a little on the one side, had a knowing bend over the right eye; one of his arms was pressed, with that peculiar affectation of carelessness which evinces care, through the rails, and brought round, so as to enable the hand to shift the coarse and bad cigar that rested on his lip – there was a torn glove upon the other; and his dull bloodshot eyes winked impudently upon every girl that passed.'

**Learn, teach** A matter which used to wound the tender sensibilities of my teachers long ago was the inability to distinguish between *learn* and *teach*. To hear things like 'my mother learned me that poem', used to make them wince, poor things. It was considered a serious grammatical error.

Well now, a man generally considered to be worth a pass mark in English wrote, 'A thousand more mischances than this one have learn'd me how to brook this patiently', in *Two Gentlemen of Verona*. So what we hear all over the place in Ireland is hardly bad English. Now the origin of *learn* is Old English *leornian*, to study, to learn; it did not then mean to teach. But later on, in the Middle English period, *learn* came to mean teach as well, and was considered correct until the eighteenth century when the new, prescriptive grammarians decided to describe both Spenser's and Shakespeare's use of learn as 'illiterate'.

Dr Johnson in his dictionary (1755) was kinder

than the grammarians. Thinking of Wyclif, perhaps, who in 1382 wrote 'Who lerneth a scornere, doth wrong he to hymself', or the *York Mysteries* of c. 1440 with which he was familiar, and which has 'Thus lerned he me', Johnson simply said, 'This sense is now obsolete.' He must have known that this was not so: it was used all about him, even by his friend Malone, the great authority on Shakespeare. *Learn* derives from an ancient source which means to follow a furrow or track. Isn't that what learning is about?

**Loystering** We have many words for a good beating in Hiberno-English, but one in particular took my fancy when I first heard it. A man who lives near Dungarvan, Co. Waterford, was talking about the hooligans one meets so frequently nowadays in the streets after the public houses have closed their doors. 'The father and mother of a good loystherin' would cure most of them,' he assured me. You'll find the word in Co. Down as well, where the noun **loysther** means a good hammering. Here we have another Viking word. *Ljostra* is an Old Norse verb which means to strike.

**Me oul' segotia** I am relying on a few men from the same territory of Fingall for an explanation of the term *me oul' segotia*. Had I been sent a pound in every letter I have received over the years asking what a *segotia* was, I could go out and buy myself a villa in Tuscany. Paddy Weston of Lusk sent me a copy of hundreds of words collected by a schoolmaster, Paddy O'Neill, now alas gone to his reward. Mr O'Neill insisted that in his day the word was applied to children only, and he speculated that here we have a phrase adapted from the French by the Dublin Fusiliers who served in France during the Great War: *mon cher gosse*, my dear child.

**Mot** is a common Dublin city expression for a girl. Some say that it is a perversion of the old word *mort*, a female, a word of unknown origin. I don't think so. It comes, I think, from the Dutch *mot*, a whore, as found in the compound *mothuys*, a brothel. In the course of time Dubliners have softened the old word to mean, simply, a girl, a sweetheart. Joyce has it in *Ulysses*: 'Marie Kendall … one of them mots that do be in the packets of fags.' Brendan Behan sang: 'We went up there on our honeymoon;/ Said the mot to me "if you don't come soon,/ I'll have to get in with the hairy baboon/ Up in the Zoological Gardens."'

**Potwalloper** Gone are the days when an Irish hotel could advertise in the local papers for a *potwalloper*. I can assure you that I have seen one such a notice in my time, in a southern rural paper which once gained a certain notoriety from warning the Czar of Russia that it had its eye on him. The word means a kitchen worker of low grade, such as a dishwasher. This is an old word, imported from England perhaps in medieval times. Formerly it meant a man who qualified as a voter in some English borough by having a separate fireplace in which he could boil his very own meat. The word is an alteration of the earlier *potwaller*, from *pot*, plus *waller*, from *wall*, to boil, from Old English *weallan*. The formation of the word as we now know it was probably influenced by the dialect *wallop*, to boil hard. Nothing at all to do with beating the utensils.

**Saint Fairy Anne** Here we have another soldiers' phrase. I've heard it said in north county Dublin by a woman to a friend who had spilled his tea over her pretty table cloth. By *Saint Fairy Anne* she meant something like 'It doesn't matter', or 'Don't worry about it.' She didn't speak French. Had she done so she would have said *cela ne fait rien*. And don't blame the poor soldiers of the Dublin Fusiliers for making a hash of it.

**Scran** This word is commonly heard in Ireland in the minor curse **Bad scran to you!** Here in Wicklow, *scran* means loose change, unmarketable fish, as well as scraps of food. I once believed in the theory that scran is from Icelandic *skran*, refuse, rubbish; but I must tell you that the Oxford Dictionary has now discarded this theory. It is probably coincidental, it says. It offers no alternative.

**She was in a pottle of tears.** I've often heard this expression in Cork to describe a fair old weep. I haven't come across it elsewhere. *Pottle* has not yet been consigned to the dialect dictionaries, but I'm told on good authority that it is on its way there. It was formerly a liquid measure equal to two quarts; then it came to mean a pot or tankard holding two quarts; then the liquid in such a pot; then booze in general; then any small container, such as a strawberry punnet. 'I'll give you a pottle of burned sack,' says Ford to the Hostess in *The Merry Wives of Windsor*. Shakespeare also refers to a *pottle-pot* in *Henry IV*, part 2. '*Shallow*: By the mass you'll crack a quart together, ha! will you not, Master Bardolph? *Bardolph*: Yes, sir, in a pottle-pot.' *Pottle* is from Old French *potel*, a diminutive, from *pot*, pot, from Vulgar Latin *pottus*.

**Shillelaghs** were what the cudgels used in the serious faction fights were called. The word has nothing whatever to do with the village of Shillelagh in Co. Wicklow, which happened to have been surrounded with impressive oak woods, cut down, alas, to provide timber for halls and palaces from South Africa to London in the eighteenth century, and to provide planking for Britain's fleet. No, contrary to what the dictionaries may tell you, shillelagh, the cudgel, is from the Irish **sail éille**. *Sail* is a cudgel; *éille* is the genitive case of *iall*, a thong, by which the fighting man secured the weapon to his wrist. The Irish compound is found in many eighteenth-century songs and poems, and the Anglo-Irish *shillelagh* is close to the pronunciation of the original Irish.

**Sowl** Some words have flummoxed generations of lexicographers. Nobody knows where the good south Tipperary and Waterford word *sowl* comes from. It means to pull by the ears. It is in common dialect use in England. Shakespeare knew it. He has 'He'll go, he says, and sowl the porter of Rome gates by the ears', in *Coriolanus*.

**Starms** Many's the strange word I have heard over the years from old sailors and old fishermen who have drifted in and out of ports between Yarmouth and Dunmore East. One such word is *starms*, sent to me by an old man from Killybegs, Co. Donegal. Starms, he told me, are what we landlubbers call stars.

Yes, *starms* are seen all over England's north country, and in Scotland as well. 'There's a heaven aboon us a', and a bonny moon an' sterns in it,' wrote Scott in *The Heart of Midlothian*. So the word is not confined to fishermen. I know that some Donegal sheepmen have given the name *starna* to a ewe having a white spot on its brow; and, like the seamen, they talk of *starless nights* here and there among the Blue Stacks. The *n* in *starn* is influenced by Old Norse *stjarna*. *Star*, incidentally, has its origin in Old English *steorra*. I plead justification in including *starms* in this section, rather than in the Ulster section, because I heard it from two people in my own town of New Ross, Co. Wexford; one was an old man, Henry Browne, who sailed the seven seas on the four-riggers; the other was my grandmother, Mary Kate Payne, whose people for generations back were also seafarers.

**Stim** This good word, often written **styme** or **stime**, has been relegated to dialect status in many dictionaries. It is in general use in Irish dialects, as well as in the dialects of Scotland and northern England. It means the faintest form of any object; a glimpse or gleam of light. 'I scarce could wink to see a styme,' wrote Burns in *There's Naethin Like the Honest Nappy*, which is a paean to ale, not to motherhood. Our own Charles Lever wrote, 'The night was dark … you could not see a stim,' in *Charles O'Malley*. Not far from Glenties in Co. Donegal I once heard an old woman speak of a furtive look or glance as a *styme*. In an 1829 Scottish songbook I once bought for half a crown, there is the same shade of meaning: 'I see him in aside the bink (*bench*)/ I gae him bread an ale to drink,/ An ne'er a blythe styme wad he blink …' In Scotland the adjective *stimey* means dim-sighted. There is also the noun *stimey* which means one who is clumsy because of impaired eyesight. Hence the golfing term *stymie*, the predicament in which a player was placed when he found his opponent's ball lying in the line of his putt. The wicked stymie rule, if revived, would, I feel, make professional golf more interesting, and might even take the smile off the face of the Tiger. Anyway, *stime, stime* and *styme* are from the Old Norse *skima*, a gleam of light.

**Stroke** My father was fond of this word. Whenever he wanted to praise a child for eating up, he invariably used **stroke** for appetite: 'He has a great stroke, God bless him.' The word is to be found in many Irish counties. It first appears in literature in 1699 in a book by William Dampier called *A New Voyage Around the World*. He wrote: 'Neither can any man be entertain'd as a soldier, that has not a greater stroke than ordinary at eating.' Swift had the word as well; but after him not a trace of this stroke may be found in English literature. The Dean wrote in *Polite Conversation*: 'Lady: God bless you, Colonel, you have a good stroke with you.' I have found the word in a nineteenth-century glossary from Northumberland: 'The bairn, he's a grand stroke', meaning the child has a good appetite. Not a trace of it elsewhere. I suppose it came from Middle English *strók*, like all the other strokes found in English, and this word represents Old English *strák*. The related Dutch has *streek*, and modern German *streich*.

**Strollop** I heard this word from a Traveller. He was talking horses as usual. He wouldn't take a present of a certain racehorse, he told me, because he was an oul' strollop. A strollop, he explained, is a horse with a lazy, aimless walk in the parade ring. The word is not in any of the Irish dialect glossaries, as far as I know, but I found it in a glossary from Lancashire. 'A slovenly, untidy walker', says one. It is also a verb in that county. But where does my friend's word originate? The dictionaries shy away. I would guess that it is a fusion of *trollop*, ultimately from Old French *troller*, a hunting term, 'to hunt to no purpose', and *stroll*, an early seventeenth-century borrowing from the High German, introduced to English by soldiers; compare the German *strolch*, a vagabond. Where did our nomads get the word? God only knows.

**Tack** By far the most interesting word I've heard in recent years is one I heard in west Co. Waterford as the foot-and-mouth epidemic raged in England. 'God keep that tack from us,' a farmer from the foothills of the Comeragh mountains said of the plague. From French *tac* this, 'a kind of rot among sheep, also a plague spot', according to Randle Cotgrave's French-English dictionary of 1610. The French word is from the Latin *tactus*, found in the sense infectious, contagious disease.

**Teach** is from Old English *taecan*, to show.
What a wonderful survival is the Barony of Forth,
Co. Wexford, *teach*, used in phrases such as **teach
me the salt**, which means show me, pass it to me.
They pronounce it *taych*.

**Whelm** is a word you may hear along Ireland's
east coast. We all use it combined with *over-*, of
course, but it is a good old word in its own right.
I first heard whelm from an old Arklowman who
had many years earlier retired from a life at sea.
I have heard it, too, from old Wexford seamen.
The great dictionaries give the word's primary
meaning as 'to submerge', but most ignore the
word's shades of meaning in dialect.

An old Wicklow stonemason explained that to
whelm means to cover something up, bags of
cement with a tarpaulin, for example. This, too,
was the explanation given to me by the old salts
I heard the word from. Jehan Palsgrave's French-
English dictionary of 1530 has 'I whelme it, to
save it from the flyes.' This meaning is still found
in Scotland and in England as far south as Suffolk.
A Peterborough woman is recorded in the *English
Dialect Dictionary* as having said that she had seven
children so small that she could whelm them all
under a basket.

*Whelm* is from late Old English *hwylfan* = Old
Norse *hvelfa*, to arch, vault, turn upside down. A
tract from c. 1340 has 'welme the cuppe'.

**Wildfire** 'The foot-and-mouth disease will spread like wildfire here if it reaches us,' said a neighbour's child to me as we watched thousands of sheep being rounded up for slaughter; immediately she added, 'What's wildfire anyway?' It is the will-o'-the-wisp, phosphorescence occasioned by dying vegetation, often seen on boglands and always at night, as you'll know.

Summer lightning is called *wildfire* in Scotland, and I've heard Irish trawlermen use the word in this context. Burns has 'Was't the wildfire scorched their boughs?' in *Verses near Drumlanrig*.

It was also a name for erysipilas, both in south-east Ireland and in south-western England, from where it probably reached us. 'A wilde fyr up-on their bodies fall!' wrote old Chaucer.

A little book I bought for £1 in Cornwall, Hunt's *Popular Romances of the West of England*, has this little charm against erysipilas: 'Christ he walketh over the land,/ Carried the wildfire in his hand./ He rebuked the fire and bid it stand/ In the name of the Father and of the Son, and of the Holy Ghost.' Alas, there is no charm against the foot-and-mouth disease that I know of.